ASCENT®
CENTER FOR TECHNICAL KNOWLEDGE

ENOVIA V5-6R2017:
DMU Fitting Simulator

Learning Guide
1ˢᵗ Edition

ASCENT - Center for Technical Knowledge®
ENOVIA V5-6R2017: DMU Fitting Simulator
1st Edition

Prepared and produced by:

ASCENT Center for Technical Knowledge
630 Peter Jefferson Parkway, Suite 175
Charlottesville, VA 22911

866-527-2368
www.ASCENTed.com

Lead Contributor: Scott Hendren

ASCENT - Center for Technical Knowledge is a division of Rand Worldwide, Inc., providing custom developed knowledge products and services for leading engineering software applications. ASCENT is focused on specializing in the creation of education programs that incorporate the best of classroom learning and technology-based training offerings.

We welcome any comments you may have regarding this student guide, or any of our products. To contact us please email: feedback@ASCENTed.com.

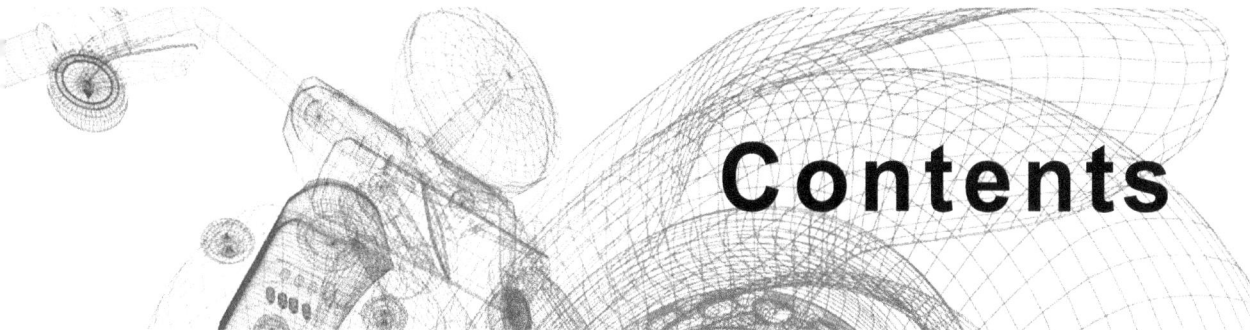

Contents

Preface

The *ENOVIA V5-6R2017: DMU Fitting Simulator* student guide enables you to simulate the assembly and dis-assembly of components. These simulations are analyzed for clash and minimum distances to determine whether the assembly process is realistic. Also, swept volumes are developed to visualize clash conditions. Finally, the path finder tool is used to modify a track to avoid a clash condition.

Topics Covered:

- Introduction to the DMU Fitting workbench.

- Creating a shuttle.

- Creating a track and modifying track operators.

- Generating a sequence.

- Creating a replay and video.

- Creating a swept volume.

- Using Space Analysis tools such as clash and distance and band analysis.

- Using the path finder to optimize a track.

Note on Software Setup

This student guide assumes a standard installation of the software using the default preferences during installation. Lectures and practices use the standard software templates and default options for the Content Libraries.

Lead Contributor: Scott Hendren

Scott Hendren has been a trainer and curriculum developer in the PLM industry for over 20 years, with experience on multiple CAD systems, including Pro/ENGINEER, Creo Parametric, and CATIA. Trained in Instructional Design, Scott uses his skills to develop instructor-led and web-based training products.

Scott has held training and development positions with several high profile PLM companies, and has been with the Ascent team since 2013.

Scott holds a Bachelor of Mechanical Engineering Degree as well as a Bachelor of Science in Mathematics from Dalhousie University, Nova Scotia, Canada.

Scott Hendren has been the Lead Contributor for *ENOVIA: DMU Fitting Simulator* since 2013.

In this Guide

The following images highlight some of the features that can be found in this guide.

Practice Files

The Practice Files page tells you how to download and install the practice files that are provided with this guide.

Link to the practice files

Chapters

Each chapter begins with a brief introduction and a list of the chapter's Learning Objectives.

Learning Objectives for the chapter

Side notes

Side notes are hints or additional information for the current topic.

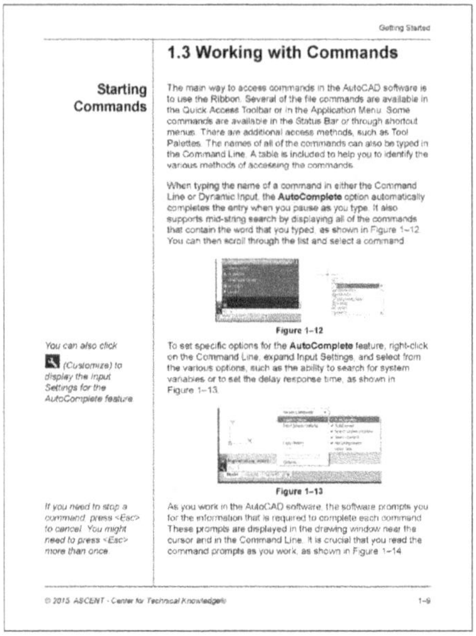

Getting Started

1.3 Working with Commands

Starting Commands

The main way to access commands in the AutoCAD software is to use the Ribbon. Several of the file commands are available in the Quick Access Toolbar or in the Application Menu. Some commands are available in the Status Bar or through shortcut menus. There are additional access methods, such as Tool Palettes. The names of all of the commands can also be typed in the Command Line. A table is included to help you to identify the various methods of accessing the commands.

When typing the name of a command in either the Command Line or Dynamic Input, the **AutoComplete** option automatically completes the entry when you pause as you type. It also supports mid-string search by displaying all of the commands that contain the word that you typed, as shown in Figure 1–12. You can then scroll through the list and select a command.

Figure 1–12

You can also click (Customize) to display the Input Settings for the AutoComplete feature.

To set specific options for the **AutoComplete** feature, right-click on the Command Line, expand Input Settings, and select from the various options, such as the ability to search for system variables or to set the delay response time, as shown in Figure 1–13.

Figure 1–13

If you need to stop a command, press <Esc> to cancel. You might need to press <Esc> more than once.

As you work in the AutoCAD software, the software prompts you for the information that is required to complete each command. These prompts are displayed in the drawing window near the cursor and in the Command Line. It is crucial that you read the command prompts as you work, as shown in Figure 1–14.

© 2015 ASCENT - Center for Technical Knowledge® 1–9

Instructional Content

Each chapter is split into a series of sections of instructional content on specific topics. These lectures include the descriptions, step-by-step procedures, figures, hints, and information you need to achieve the chapter's Learning Objectives.

Practice Objectives

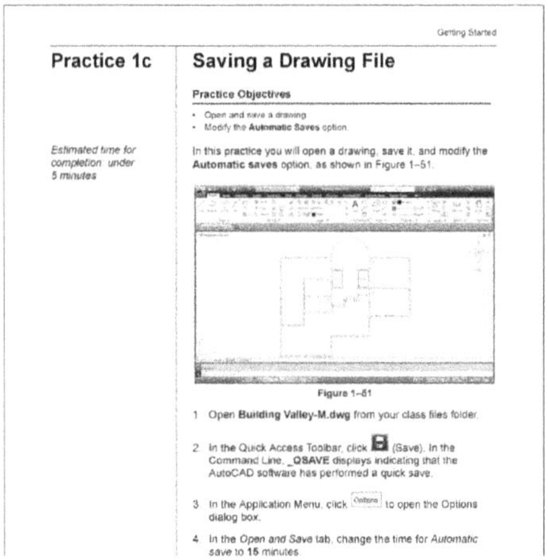

Getting Started

Practice 1c — Saving a Drawing File

Practice Objectives

- Open and save a drawing.
- Modify the **Automatic Saves** option.

Estimated time for completion: under 5 minutes

In this practice you will open a drawing, save it, and modify the **Automatic saves** option, as shown in Figure 1–51.

Figure 1–51

1. Open **Building Valley-M.dwg** from your class files folder.
2. In the Quick Access Toolbar, click (Save). In the Command Line, **_QSAVE** displays indicating that the AutoCAD software has performed a quick save.
3. In the Application Menu, click Options to open the Options dialog box.
4. In the *Open and Save* tab, change the time for *Automatic save* to **15** minutes.

Practices

Practices enable you to use the software to perform a hands-on review of a topic.

Some practices require you to use prepared practice files, which can be downloaded from the link found on the Practice Files page.

Practice Files

To download the practice files for this guide, use the following steps:

1. Type the URL shown below into the address bar of your Internet browser. The URL must be typed **exactly as shown**. If you are using an ASCENT ebook, you can click on the link to download the file.

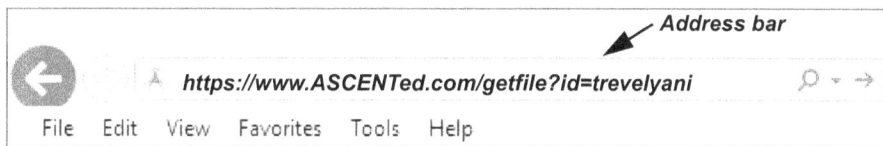

Address bar

https://www.ASCENTed.com/getfile?id=trevelyani

File Edit View Favorites Tools Help

2. Press <Enter> to download the .ZIP file that contains the Practice Files.

3. Once the download is complete, unzip the file to a local folder. The unzipped file contains an .EXE file.

4. Double-click on the .EXE file and follow the instructions to automatically install the Practice Files on the C:\ drive of your computer.

    Do not change the location in which the Practice Files folder is installed. Doing so can cause errors when completing the practices.

https://www.ASCENTed.com/getfile?id=trevelyani

Stay Informed!

Interested in receiving information about upcoming promotional offers, educational events, invitations to complimentary webcasts, and discounts? If so, please visit:

www.ASCENTed.com/updates/

Help us improve our product by completing the following survey:

www.ASCENTed.com/feedback

You can also contact us at: *feedback@ASCENTed.com*

Introduction to DMU Fitting Simulator

The DMU Fitting Simulator is used to simulate the assembly or disassembly of components in an assembly. In this chapter, you will review the DMU Fitting simulator user interface and tools available in the DMU Fitting Simulator workbench.

Learning Objectives in this Chapter

- Conduct an overview pf the DMU Fitting Simulator.
- Recognize and use the DMU Fitting tools.

1.1 DMU Fitting Simulator

The DMU Fitting workbench is used to accomplish the following tasks:

- Simulate assembly or disassembly of components in an assembly.

- Generate replays and video files.

- Perform clash analyses.

- Perform distance and band analyses.

- Create swept volumes.

- Explode an assembly.

- Perform a path analysis to derive the optimum assembly or disassembly path.

- Monitor model measurements during the assembly or disassembly process and report measurement values to a text file or spreadsheet.

To access the DMU Fitting workbench, select **Start>Digital Mockup>DMU Fitting**. The DMU Fitting interface opens as shown in Figure 1–1.

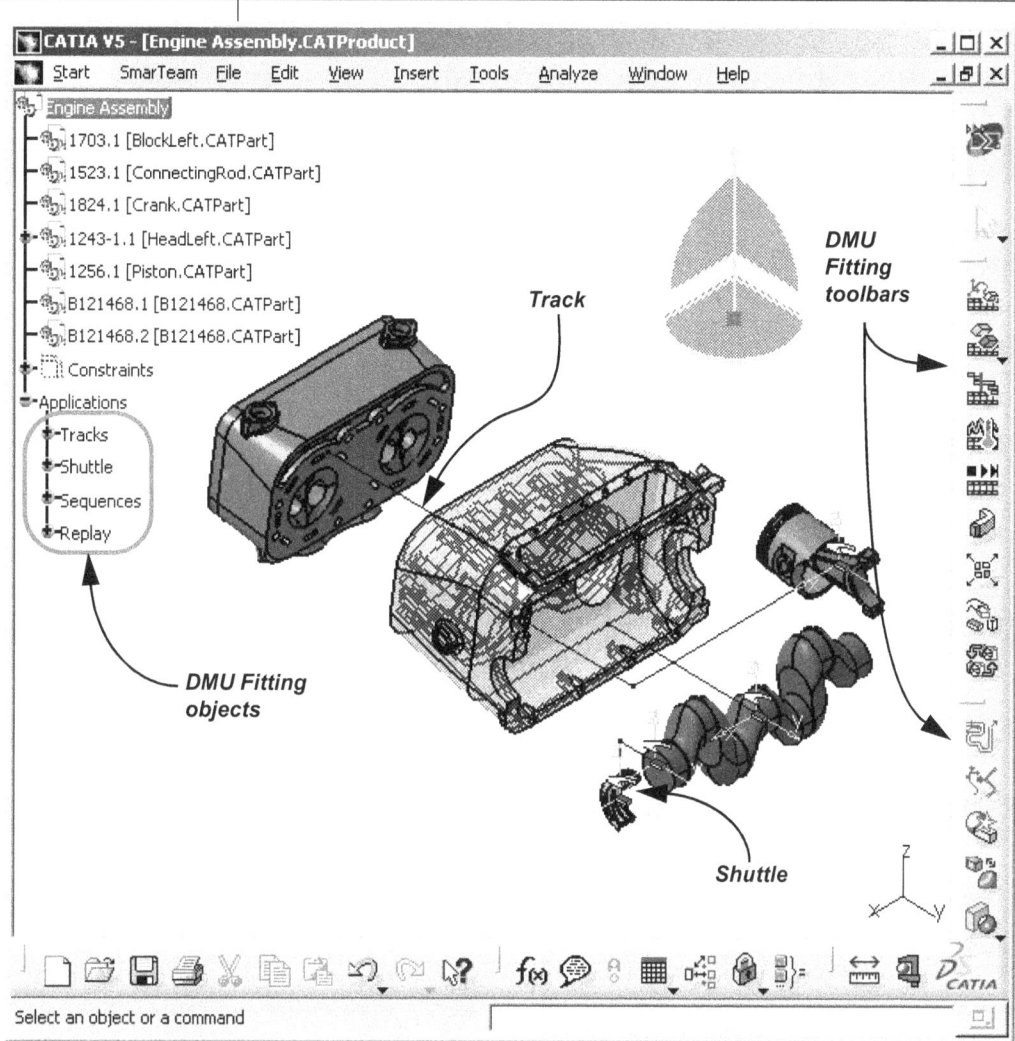

CATIA V5 - [Engine Assembly.CATProduct]

Start   SmarTeam   File   Edit   View   Insert   Tools   Analyze   Window   Help

Engine Assembly
— 1703.1 [BlockLeft.CATPart]
— 1523.1 [ConnectingRod.CATPart]
— 1824.1 [Crank.CATPart]
— 1243-1.1 [HeadLeft.CATPart]
— 1256.1 [Piston.CATPart]
— B121468.1 [B121468.CATPart]
— B121468.2 [B121468.CATPart]
— Constraints
— Applications
  — Tracks
  — Shuttle
  — Sequences
  — Replay

DMU Fitting objects

Track

DMU Fitting toolbars

Shuttle

Select an object or a command

Figure 1–1

1.2 DMU Fitting Tools

This section provides an overview of the different tools available in the DMU Fitting Simulator workbench.

The workbench consists of two main toolbars and a drop-down list:

- DMU Simulation Toolbar
- DMU Check Toolbar
- Simulation drop-down list

DMU Simulation Toolbar

The DMU Simulation toolbar opens as shown in Figure 1–2. The tools are described in the table below.

Figure 1–2

Icon	Option		Description
	Track		Records and replays the motion of an object.
	Generate Track		Creates the track using the edges of the model.
	Other Actions flyout		
		Color Action	Controls the color of an object. Color changes are recorded and can be replayed.
		Visibility Action	Controls the visibility of an object. Visibility changes are recorded and can be replayed.
	Edit Sequence		A sequence is a combination of tracks, color actions, visibility actions, and other previously defined sequences. The order and duration of each action can be customized.

Icon	Option	Description
	Edit & Perform Experiment	Enables you to record the value of a sensor (such as a measurement) over the duration of a track, sequence, or replay. The results of an experiment provide numerical data that can be saved in a text file or Excel spreadsheet.
	Simulation Player	Opens a Player toolbar that enables you to play or replay a sequence. It typically runs more quickly than directly accessing the sequence or replay.
	Swept Volume	Creates a representation of the volume consumed by an object as it travels along the length of a track. The volume can be saved as a CGR file and assembled into the product.
	Explode	Explodes the components of an assembly.
	Shuttle	A group of components that is used to create a track, color action, or visibility action for more than one component.
	Reset Position	Resets all assembly components to their positions before a track, sequence, or replay was run.

DMU Check Toolbar

The DMU Check toolbar opens as shown in Figure 1–3. The tools in this toolbar are described in the table below.

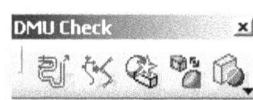

Figure 1–3

Icon	Option	Description
	Path Finder	Uses an existing track to define the start and end point. The system creates a new path that moves the object from start to end without interfering with any other assembly components or leaving a predefined bounding box. This results in a new track that consists of a series of sampling points connected by lines.

	Smooth		Used to improve the quality of an existing track. This is most useful on a track created by the path finder since the end result is a series of connected lines.
	Clash		Run a clash analysis on the product using the current component positions and orientations.
	Distance and Band Analysis		Run a distance and band analysis on the product using the current component positions and orientations.
	Automatic Clash Detection flyout		These icons are used to determine how the system reacts to a clash when a track, sequence, or replay is simulated.
		Off	No clash analysis is performed.
		On	A clash analysis is performed. When a clash is detected, the affected areas are highlighted in red.
		Stop	A clash analysis is performed. When a clash is detected, the affected areas are highlighted in red and the simulation is stopped.

Simulation Drop-Down List

The Simulation drop-down list is accessed by selecting **Tools> Simulation**, as shown in Figure 1–4.

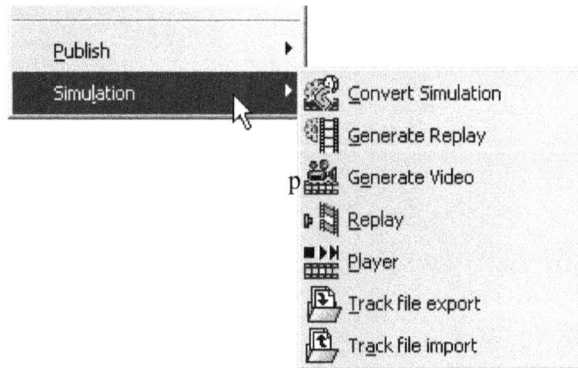

Figure 1–4

These options are described as follows:

Icon	Option	Description
	Convert Simulation	Simulations can be generated using a variety of DMU workbenches. This option enables you to convert the motion generated by the simulation into a track that can be used in a sequence in the DMU Fitting Simulator workbench.
	Generate Replay	Create a replay of a sequence. A replay typically runs more quickly than a sequence. It can only be run in the DMU workbenches.
	Generate Video	Record a track, sequence, or replay to a Microsoft AVI, Microsoft MPEG, or Still Image Capture file. A video can be replayed without a DMU license.
	Replay	Used to watch a replay. Replays can also be reviewed by double-clicking on them in the specification tree.
	Player	Opens a Player toolbar that enables you to play or replay a sequence. This is the same as ▪▶▶ (Simulation Player) in the DMU Simulation toolbar.
	Track file export	Save existing track(s) to an XML file that can be re-imported into the product. This is a useful tool when testing a number of different assembly or disassembly scenarios.
	Track file import	Used to import an existing XML track file into the current product.

1.3 Work in Fitting Simulator

This section provides a general overview of the steps that are required to prepare, simulate, and analyze a product in the DMU Fitting Simulator.

General Steps

Use the following general steps to use the DMU Fitting Simulator:

1. Access the DMU Fitting workbench.
2. Record component movement.
3. Define and record a simulation.
4. Apply analysis tools.

Step 1 - Access the DMU Fitting workbench.

To access the DMU Fitting workbench, select **Start>Digital Mockup>DMU Fitting**. If a CATProduct model is not already opened, a new file is created for you. The workbench symbol changes to .

Step 2 - Record component movement.

The goal of the DMU Fitting workbench is to move components and record the motion of the assembly or disassembly process for playback. The movement of a component is defined using a track. Each track enables you to move an object along a path using the compass and then record this path into the track. An object can be a single component or group of components defined using a shuttle.

For example, the assembly shown in Figure 1–5 displays two tracks. The linear track is created by referencing the **Upper Swingarm** component. The second track is created by referencing a shuttle that is comprised of the upper and lower shock housing. A variety of translational and rotational movements are combined into the track.

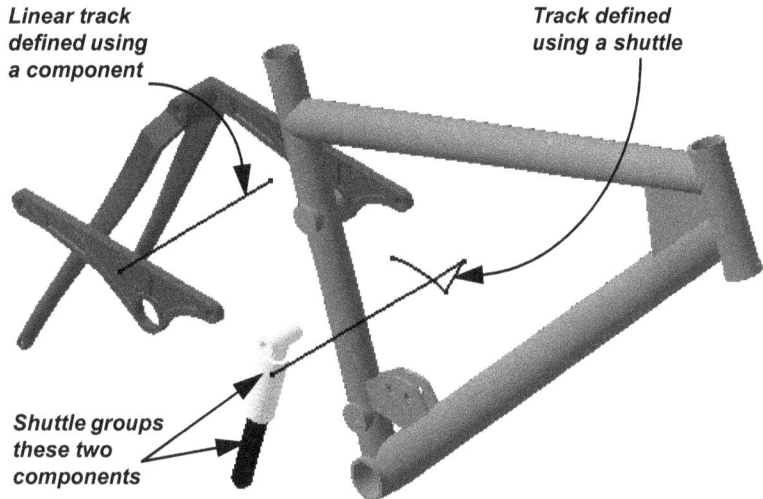

Linear track defined using a component

Track defined using a shuttle

Shuttle groups these two components

Figure 1–5

A track can also be optimized using the **Path Finder** tool or smoothed using the **Smooth** tool. These tools modify an existing track to define the required object motion for the simulation.

Step 3 - Define and record a simulation.

A simulation created in the DMU Fitting workbench enables you to review the object movements that have been defined. A simulation can be reviewed in the following ways:

- Replay a track.

- Create a sequence. This enables you to combine and control the timing of a number of tracks, color actions, and visibility actions.

- Create a replay of a track or sequence.

- Generate a video of a replay.

Step 4 - Apply analysis tools.

A variety of analysis tools are available in the DMU Fitting workbench that enable you to analyze the assembly or disassembly simulation that has been defined. These tools are described as follows:

Icon	Analysis Tool	Description	Required Input
	Swept Volume	Provides a CGR representation of the volume consumed when an object is moved along a track. The resulting CGR file can be inserted into the assembly for further analysis.	To create a swept volume, a track must be defined for the object.
	Clash	Reports the detection and value of any clash, contact, or clearance between components. The clash can be reported for a static position of assembly components or throughout the duration of a simulation.	To generate a clash analysis on the current static positions, no DMU Fitting operations are required. To report a clash for a simulation, a track, sequence, replay, or experiment is required.
	Distance and Band Analysis	Reports the minimum distance between components or graphically displays components that are within a specific distance of each other. The distance and band results can be reported for a static position of assembly components, or throughout the duration of a simulation.	To generate distance and band analysis results on the current static positions, DMU Fitting operations are not required. To report results for a simulation, a track, sequence, replay, or experiment is required.
	Edit & Perform Experiment	Reports the value of the assigned analysis results throughout the duration of a sequence. The results can be displayed in tabular or graphical format.	Any analyses that are tracked must be predefined. A sequence must also be defined that includes the required analyses.

Practice 1a

DMU Fitting Simulation

Practice Objectives

- Review the DMU Fitting features of an assembly.
- Detect a clash using a DMU Fitting replay.

In this practice, you will review the contents of a fully defined fitting simulation. The simulation reviews the assembly process of a rear-suspension mountain bike. This review is intended to introduce you to the features and functionality available in the DMU Fitting workbench.

Task 1 - Open an assembly.

1. Open **Bike.CATProduct** from the *Bike* directory. The assembly displays as shown in Figure 1–6.

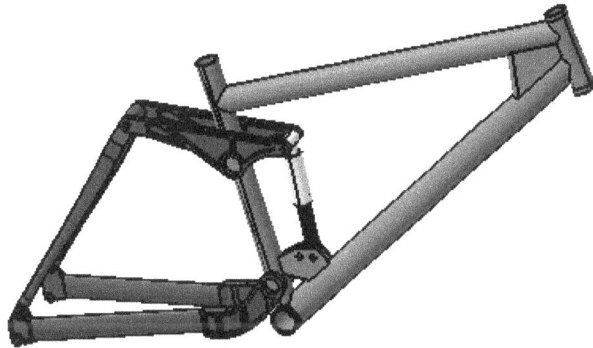

Figure 1–6

2. To access the DMU Fitting workbench, select **Start>Digital Mockup>DMU Fitting**. The workbench symbol changes to

   (Digital Mock-Up Fitting Workbench).

3. Investigate the assembly. The model contains seven components that form the frame and rear suspension system of a downhill mountain bike.

4. In the specification tree, select each component to identify it in the model.

5. In the specification tree, expand the Applications branch as shown in Figure 1–7. A number of fitting simulation features have been created including: Tracks, Shuttle, Visibility Actions, Sequences, and Replay.

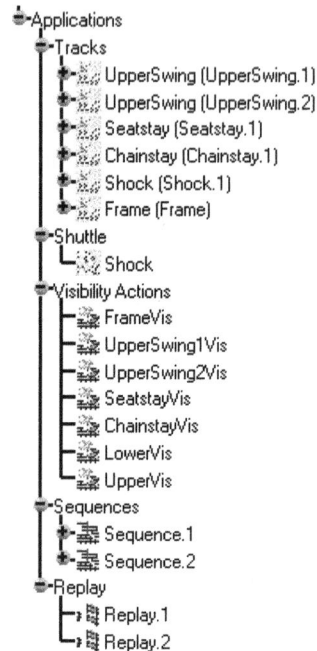

Figure 1–7

Task 2 - Review the tracks.

In this task, you will investigate the tracks that have been defined for the **Bike** assembly. Each track moves an object or shuttle through a path. The Track dialog box enables you to replay this path.

1. In the specification tree, expand the Tracks branch. Six tracks have been created.

2. In the specification tree, select the **UpperSwing (UpperSwing.1)** track.

3. Hold <Shift> and select the **Frame (Frame)** track. Doing so enables you to highlight all of the tracks in the model.

4. Right-click on all six tracks and select **Hide/Show** to display their paths as shown in Figure 1–8.

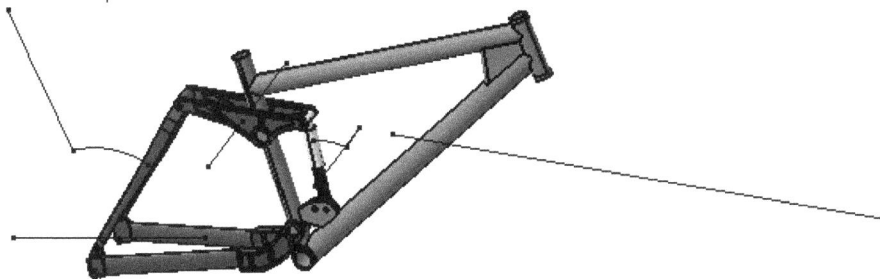

Figure 1–8

5. Double-click on the **Frame** track. The system opens the Track and Player dialog boxes. The Player dialog box shown in Figure 1–9, is used to replay the track. The system also positions the component at the starting position of the track. This track moves the **Frame** component into its assembled position.

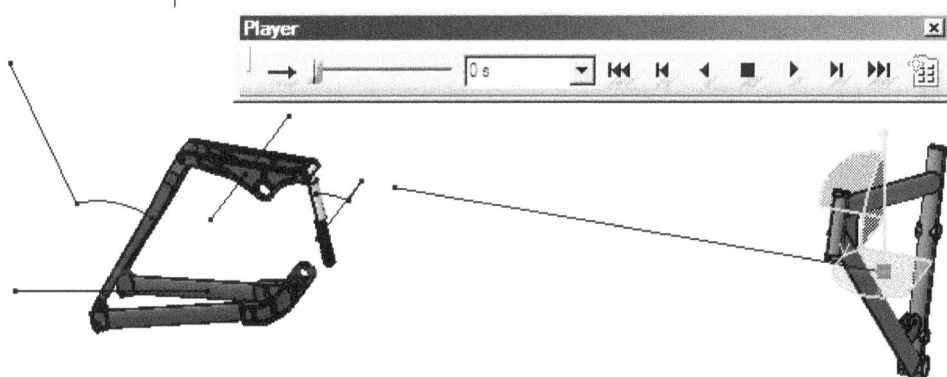

Figure 1–9

6. In the Player toolbar, click [▶] (Play Forward). The system replays the track and assembles the component.

7. Once the replay is complete, close the Track dialog box.

8. Select the other tracks and replay them. Ensure that all of the components are in their assembled positions before continuing.

Task 3 - Review the shuttle.

1. In the specification tree, expand the Shuttle branch. One shuttle has been created for this simulation.

2. Double-click on **Shock**. The Edit Shuttle and Preview dialog boxes open as shown in Figure 1–10. The purpose of this shuttle is to create a track that moves the **Lower Shock** and **Upper Shock** components together.

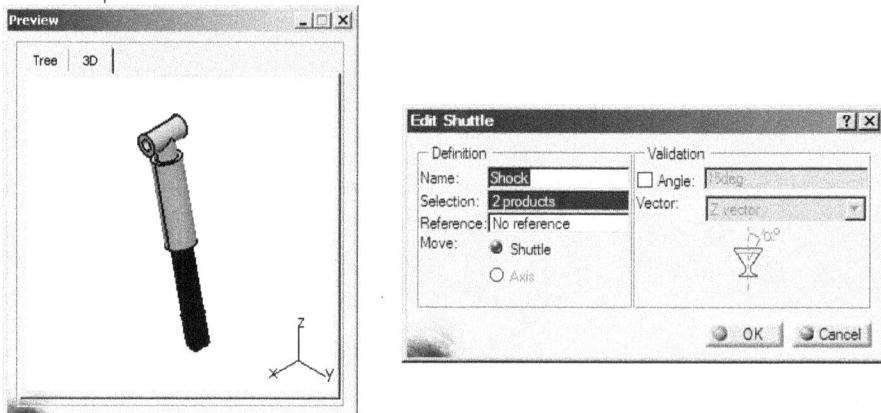

Figure 1–10

3. Close the Edit Shuttle dialog box.

Task 4 - Review the replay.

Once all of the shuttles and tracks have been defined, a sequence is generated that enables you to define the order and duration of the tracks so that they can be played back consecutively. In this task, you will review the replay that has been generated from the sequence.

1. In the specification tree, expand the Replay branch.

2. Double-click on **Replay.1**. The Replay dialog box opens as shown in Figure 1–11.

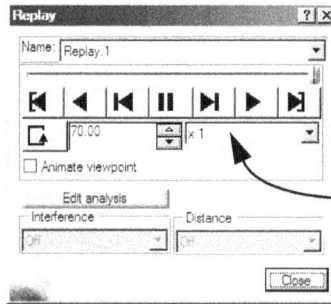

Figure 1–11

3. Click ▶ (Play Forward). The replay displays the assembly of all of the components based on their shuttles, tracks, and defined visibility actions.

4. If the speed of the playback is too slow, select an option in the Skip Ratio drop-down list to speed up the simulation.

5. Once the simulation is complete, click **Close**.

Task 5 - Check for clash on the assembly.

---

1. Double-click on **Replay.2**. Ensure that the Skip ratio is set to **x 1** and review the simulation. The sequence used to create this replay only uses the **Frame** track, which assembles the **Frame** component into the model.

2. Click ◄ (Jump to Start) to return the replay to the start.

3. In the DMU Check toolbar, in the **Clash mode** flyout, click

   (Clash Detection On), as shown in Figure 1–12.

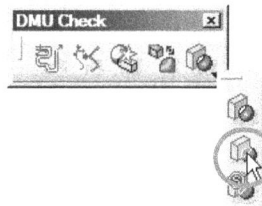

Figure 1–12

4. Replay the simulation. The system highlights any clash that occurs during the assembly of the frame component, as shown in Figure 1–13.

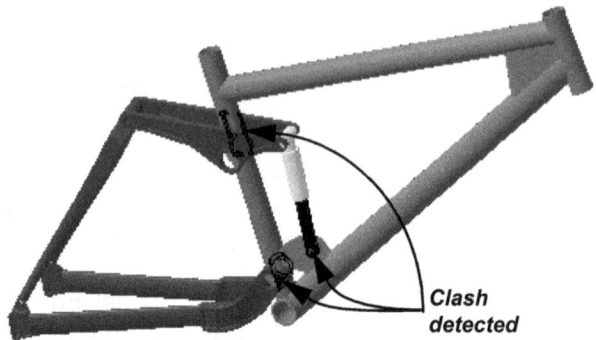

Clash detected

Figure 1–13

5. Click ![icon] (Clash Detection Stop) and replay the simulation.

6. The replay pauses at each detected clash condition. You have to keep clicking ![icon] (Play Forward) to complete the replay.

7. Replay the simulation several times while changing the value of the *Skip ratio* to **x 2**, **x 5**, and **x 10**.

Design Considerations

The simulation stops in different locations depending on the selected value of the Skip ratio. The clash detection is dependent on the size of the step taken during the replay. A larger step size might enable the system to step over a clash condition and not detect it.

8. Close all open dialog boxes.

9. Save the assembly and close the window.

Fitting Actions

In this chapter, you will learn how to create tracks, which store the recorded path of components being moved in a fitting simulation. You will also learn how to create a shuttle to define the components that are to be moved using a track.

Learning Objectives in this Chapter

- Create a Shuttle to define the components used in a track.
- Create a Track to store the recorded path of a component being moved.
- Understand the various track operations.
- Review additional Fitting actions.

2.1 Create a Shuttle

A shuttle enables you to define the component(s) to be moved using a track. Although single components can be directly selected as the object in a track, a shuttle provides additional functionality and organizational properties.

General Steps

Use the following general steps to create a shuttle:

1. Start the creation of a shuttle.
2. Select the component(s) to add to the shuttle.
3. Define additional properties for the shuttle and complete the shuttle creation.

Step 1 - Start the creation of a shuttle.

Click [icon] (Shuttle) in the DMU Simulation toolbar. The Edit Shuttle dialog box and a Preview window open as shown in Figure 2–1. Enter a descriptive name in the *Name* field.

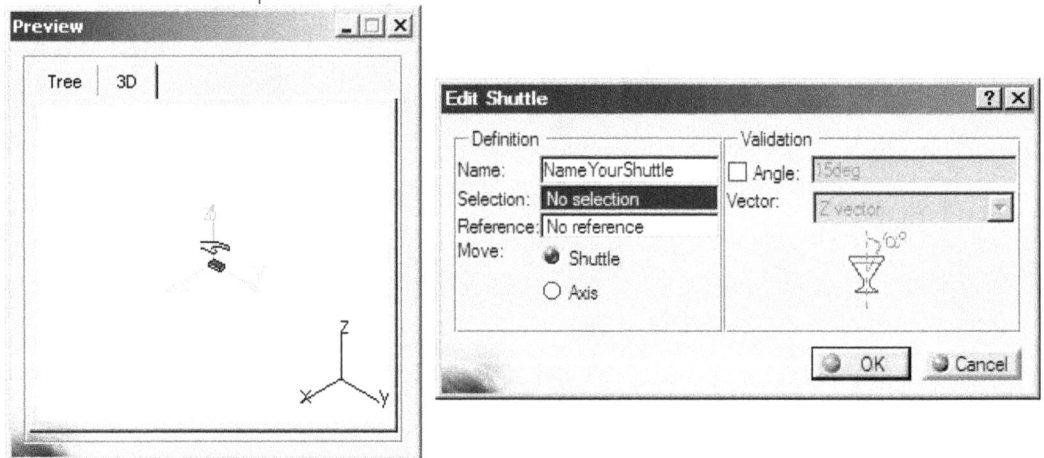

Figure 2–1

Step 2 - Select the component(s) to add to the shuttle.

To define the component(s) to add to the shuttle, select the model in the main window or specification tree. As the models are added to the shuttle, they display in the Preview window. As well, an axis system and shuttle symbol display on the models, as shown in Figure 2–2.

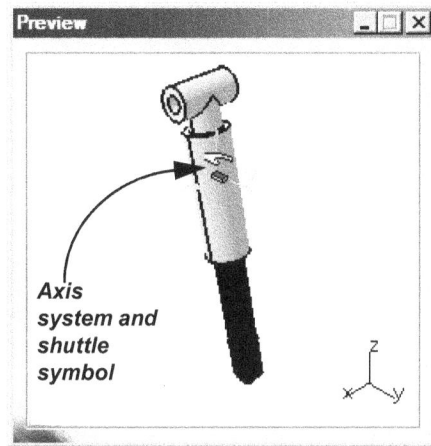

Figure 2–2

A shuttle can also be defined by selecting a predefined group or shuttle. Components can be removed from the shuttle by selecting them again.

Step 3 - Define additional properties for the shuttle and complete the shuttle creation.

The following optional properties can be defined for a shuttle:

- Reference

- Validation

Reference

When a shuttle is defined by selecting two or more shuttles, the **Reference** option determines which object is the dominant shuttle in the group. To define the reference object, select the *Reference* field and select a shuttle in the model or specification tree.

Validation

The **Validation** tool enables you to define a range of possible orientation values that are acceptable for the shuttle. This ensures that a shuttle is not oriented so that a situation, such as spilling fluid from a container, occurs during the assembly process. The defined settings are only validated during a **Path Finder** operation, which automatically generates a new path for an object so that it does not interfere with any surrounding components.

To enable **Validation** for the shuttle, select the **Angle** option and enter an acceptable angular value and vector. For example, the container shown in Figure 2–3 should not be tilted beyond 25° about the Z-vector.

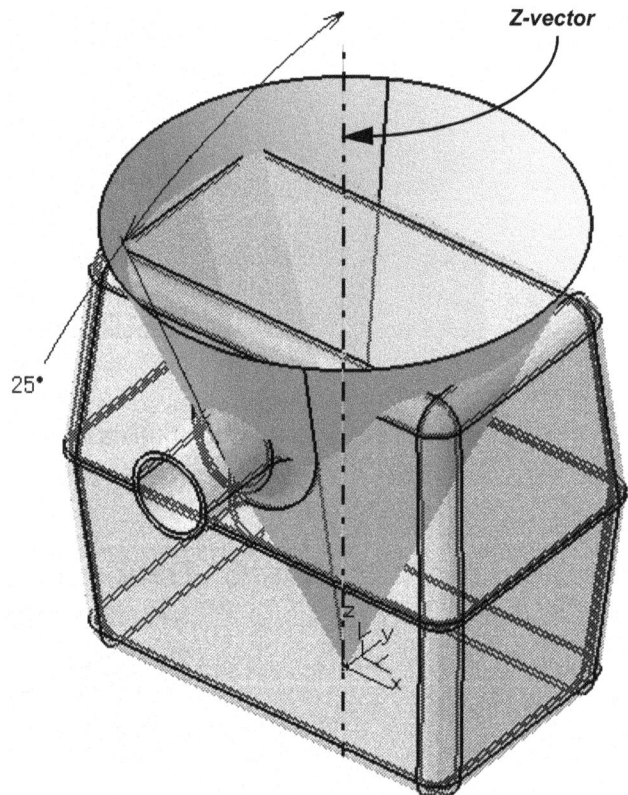

Figure 2–3

2.2 Create a Track

A track stores the recorded path of a component being moved in a fitting simulation. Any number of steps can be added to the track by recording the position and orientation of the component at each new location into the track. The timing for the track can be configured to reproduce the required motion.

For example, a track has been created for the **Seat Stay** component of the **Mountain Bike** product, as shown in Figure 2–4. It consists of two steps that assemble the **Seat Stay** into position. The first step translates the component downwards. The second step rotates the component to connect with the **Suspension Swing Arms**.

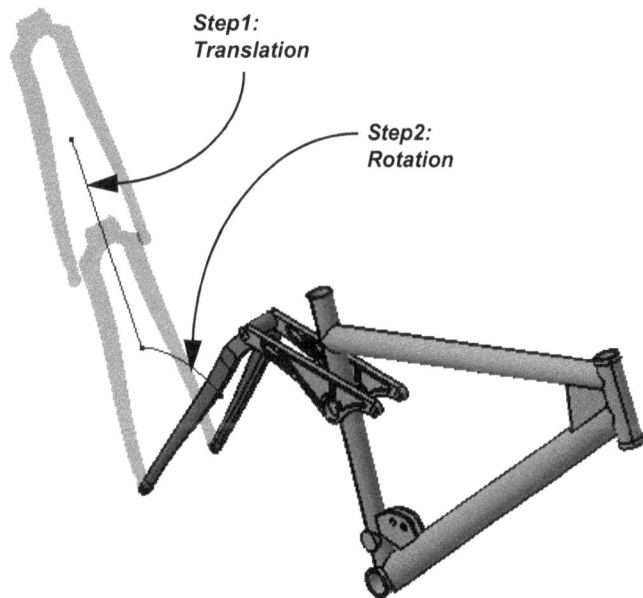

Step1:
Translation

Step2:
Rotation

Figure 2–4

General Steps

Use the following general steps to create a track:

1. Start the creation of a track.
2. Select the object to move.
3. Record the shot(s) for the track.
4. Specify optional elements and complete the track creation.

Step 1 - Start the creation of a track.

Click ▦ (Track) to open the Track dialog box as shown in Figure 2–5. Enter a name into the *Name* field. Entering a descriptive name helps you to identify the track when it is used in other areas of the Fitting Simulator workbench.

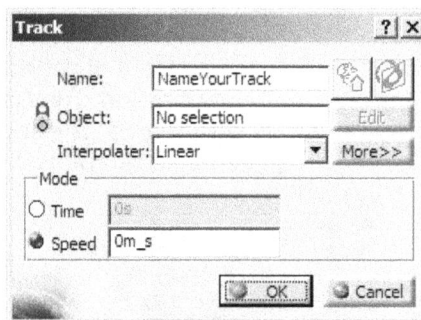

Figure 2–5

Step 2 - Select the object to move.

To define the object to move, select a component in the model or specification tree. Only a single object can be moved with a track. If more than one component is to be moved simultaneously, a shuttle must be created.

The compass is used to perform the **Move** operations. Once the object is selected, the compass automatically snaps to the object in a default position and orientation, as shown in Figure 2–6.

The compass can be repositioned on the component by dragging it to a new location.

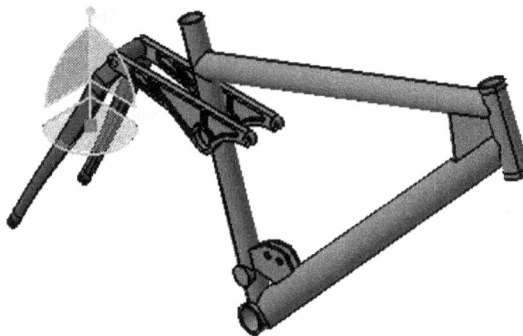

Figure 2–6

Step 3 - Record the shot(s) for the track.

How To: Record a Shot for the Track

1. Use the compass to move the object to a new orientation and/or position.

2. Click ⬛ (Record Insert) in the Recorder toolbar. The system adds the new position as a shot in the Player toolbar. By default, the Player toolbar displays the current time step for the track. The current shot can be accessed by expanding the drop-down list and selecting **Shot** as shown in Figure 2–7. Any number of **Move** operations can be stored in a single shot.

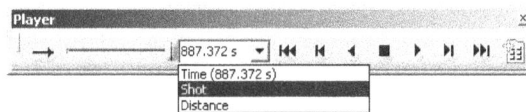

Figure 2–7

This process can be repeated to record any number of shots into a track. The shots in the track are connected by a curve, as shown in Figure 2–8.

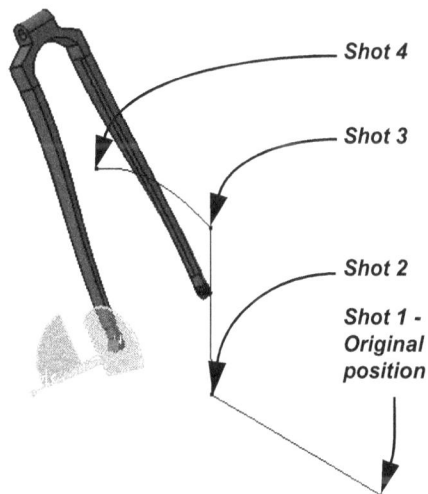

Figure 2–8

Two toolbars open when the **Track** tool is activated:

- Player toolbar

- Recorder toolbar

Player Toolbar

The Player toolbar opens as shown in Figure 2–9. It contains the standard slider and VCR controls that are used to control the playback of the track. The other options in the toolbar are described in .

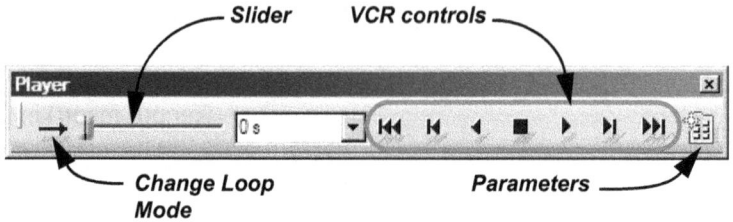

Figure 2–9

Icon	Description
(Change Loop Mode)	Enables you to change the loop mode of the player. There are three loop modes: (Single loop) (Continuous loop) (Continuous loop - reverse)
(Parameters)	The Player Parameters dialog box is used to control the step of the playback, as shown below. For example, if a track has a time of 10 seconds and a sampling step of 0.1 seconds, there are a total of 100 steps in the track. The **Temporization** option inserts a pause (defined by the value entered in seconds) between steps.

Recorder Toolbar

The Recorder toolbar opens as shown in Figure 2–10. The options in the Recorder toolbar are described in the table below.

Figure 2–10

Icon	Description
 (Record (Insert))	Inserts the current model orientation and/or position as a step in the track. When selected, the player increments to the next time step.
 (Modify)	Enables you to modify the current shot. To use this option, select a shot in the drop-down list in the Player toolbar and reposition the object using the compass. Click  to change the position of the active shot.
 (Delete)	Deletes the active shot from the track.
 (Reorder)	When selected, the Reorder Shots dialog box opens as shown below. The icons in this dialog box can be used to change the order of the shots in the track. 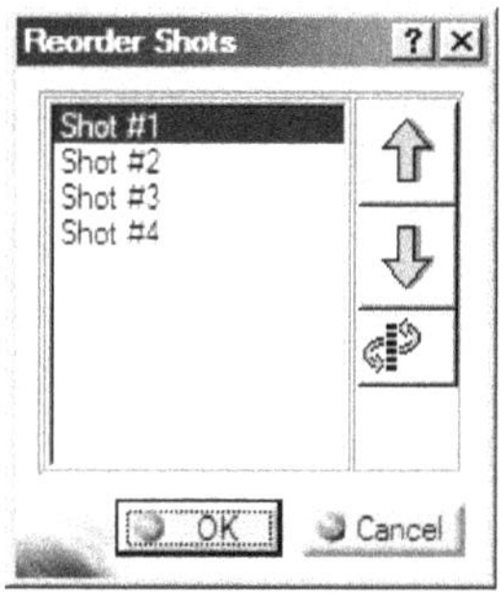

Reorder Shots ? X

Shot #1
Shot #2
Shot #3
Shot #4

⬆
⬇

OK Cancel

Icon	Description
 (Reuse Shot)	Enables you to use shots that have been saved to another track. For example, you might want the position of a bolt to match the last shot position of a track previously created for a nut. To reuse a shot, click  (Reuse Shot) and select the track from which you want to copy. The Reuse Shots dialog box opens as shown below. Select the shot that you want to reuse and click **Done**. 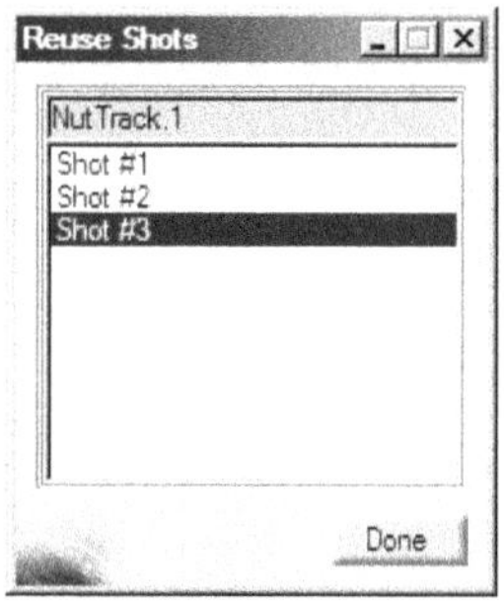

Reuse Shots _ □ X

Nut Track.1
Shot #1
Shot #2
Shot #3

Done

Step 4 - Specify optional elements and complete the track creation.

The following optional elements can be defined in the Track dialog box:

- Interpolater

- Mode

- Edit Time

Interpolator

The Interpolator drop-down list enables you to define the shape of the curve that defines the track. The three options available in the menu are described as follows:

Icon	Description
Linear	The shots are connected by lines and arcs that reproduce the path defined when creating the track exactly. An example is shown below. 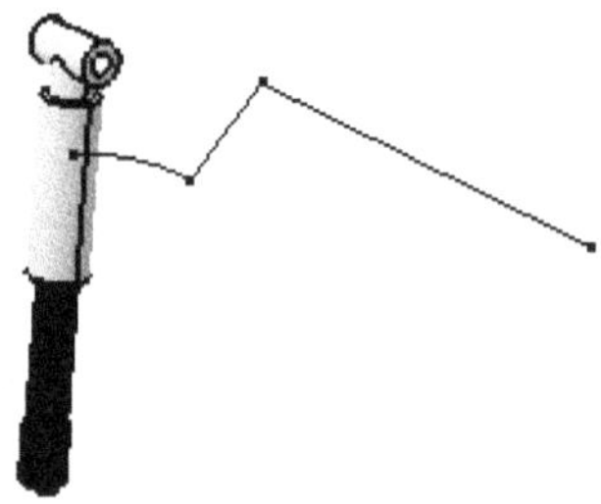
Spline	A spline curve is fitted to the shot positions. An example is shown below. 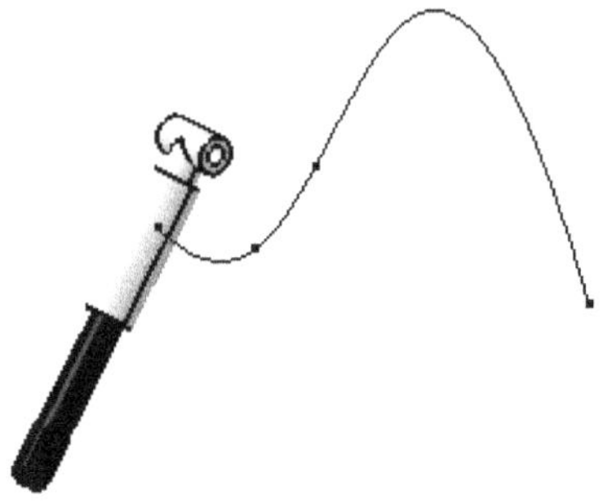

Composite Spline	The linear curve is modified using a spline to smooth the curve. An example is shown below.
	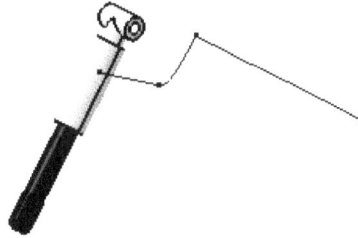

Mode

The **Mode** determines the rate of motion for the track. It can be defined using the **Time** (the duration of the track in seconds) or **Speed** (the speed of the component in units of length per second) options. By default, the system uses the **Speed** option. To define the **Mode**, select the appropriate option and enter a value, as shown in Figure 2–11.

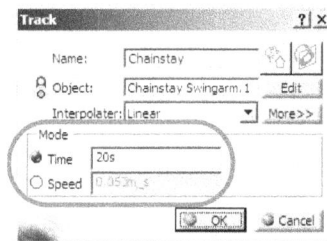

Figure 2–11

Edit Time

If more than one shot is recorded into the track, the *Edit Time* field enables you to control the relative timing of each shot. To access the *Edit Time* field, you might have to click **More**, as shown in Figure 2–12.

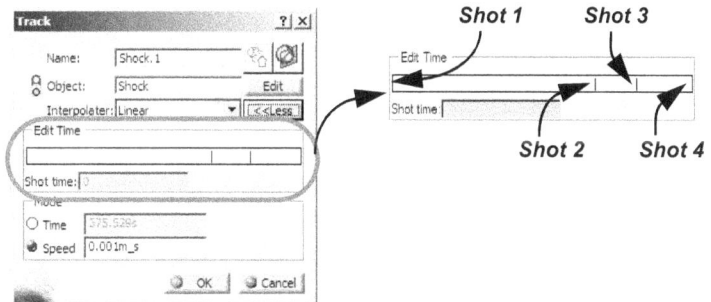

Figure 2–12

Each shot is defined by a line in the time field. If the **Time** option is used, the line can be dynamically dragged to a new position or a new time can be entered into the *Shot time* field.

Click **OK** once the definition of the track is complete. The track is added to the specification tree, as shown in Figure 2–13.

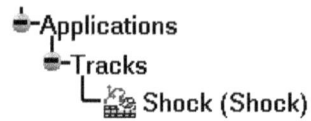

Figure 2–13

2.3 Track Operators

Access the Track dialog box by double-clicking on the track in the specification tree or on the track curve in the model. All of the properties of the track can be modified in the Track dialog box.

The following operations can be performed on a track using the shortcut menu, as shown in Figure 2–14:

- Reverse Time
- Join
- Split
- Mirror Track

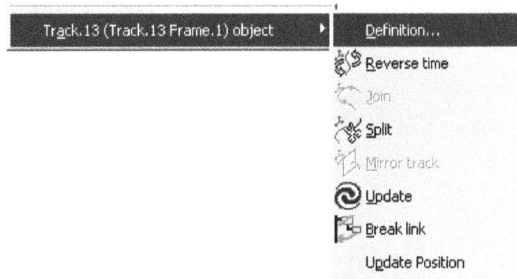

Figure 2–14

Reverse Time

The **Reverse Time** option enables you to simulate the playback of a track in reverse. This is a useful method of simulating the assembly process when starting with a fully assembled product.

When the **Reverse Time** option is selected, the system indicates the setting by placing a Reverse time branch beneath the track in the specification tree, as shown in Figure 2–15. The **Reverse Time** setting can be canceled by deleting it from the specification tree.

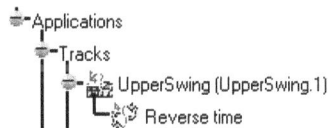

Figure 2–15

Join

The **Join** option is used to merge multiple tracks for the same object. A new track is created that contains the merged tracks.

To join two tracks, select them using <Ctrl>, right-click, and select **Selected objects>Join**. The path of the resulting track is dependant on the order in which the merged tracks were selected, as shown in Figure 2–16.

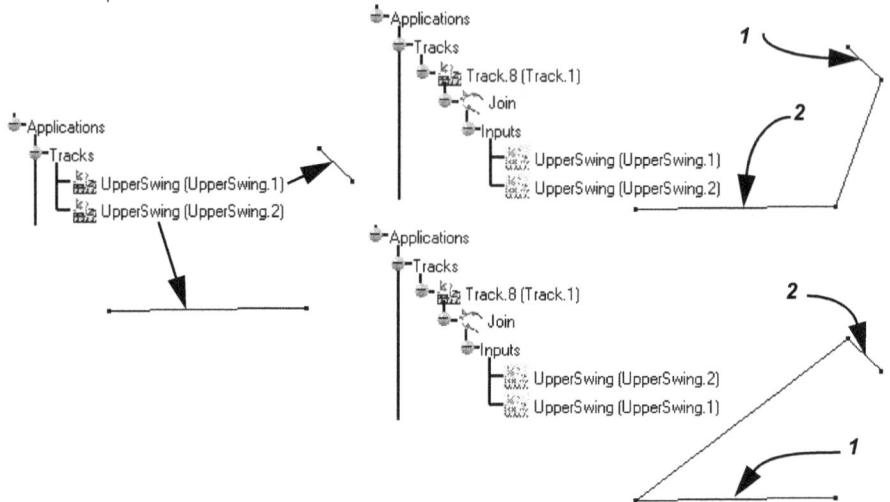

Figure 2–16

Split

The **Split** option enables you to separate a track into two tracks based on the selection of a dividing point or segment. To split a track, right-click and select **Track object>Split**. Then select a point or segment to divide the track. When a segment is selected, two discontinuous tracks are created, as shown in Figure 2–17.

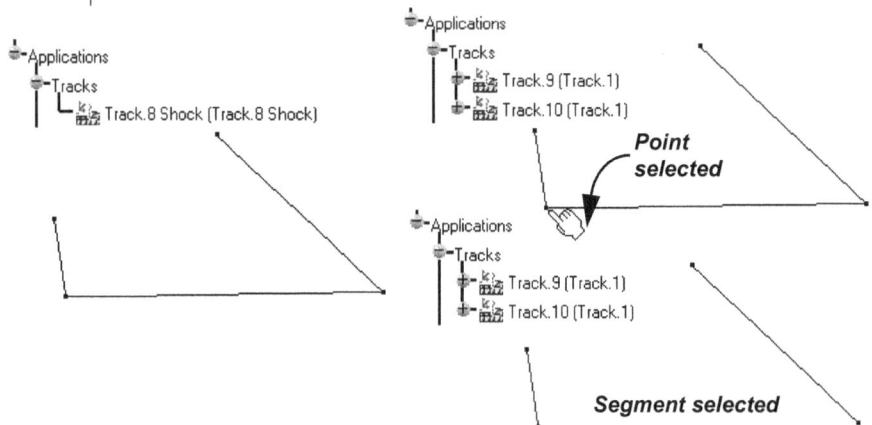

Figure 2–17

Mirror Track

The **Mirror Track** option is used to mirror an existing track about the UV plane of the compass.

How To: Mirror a Track

1. Position the compass so that the UV plane is located at the required symmetry plane.
2. Right-click and select **Track Object>Mirror Track**. A new track is created that is a non-associative mirror of the referenced track.

An example is shown in Figure 2–18.

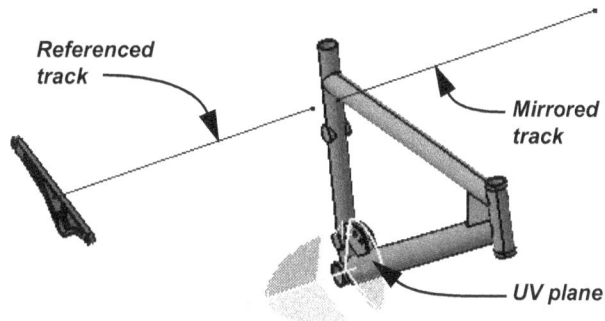

Figure 2–18

2.4 Include Additional Fitting Actions

In addition to tracks, the following fitting actions can be included in a fitting simulation:

- Color Action
- Visibility Action
- Explode

Color Action

How To: Modify an Object's Color During a Simulation

1. In the DMU Simulation toolbar, click [icon] (Color Action). The Color Action dialog box opens as shown in Figure 2–19.

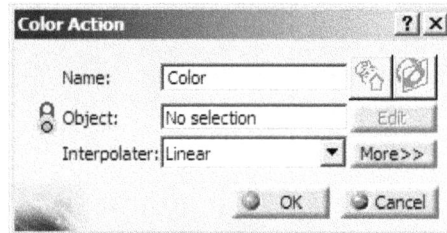

Figure 2–19

2. Select an object. It can be a component or shuttle. Once an object is selected, the Properties toolbar opens (if it is not already displayed) so that a new color can be selected for the object.
3. Enter a name for the color action.
4. In the Graphics Properties toolbar, expand the drop-down list and select a new color.

5. Click [icon] (Record Insert) to insert a shot.
6. Repeat Steps 4 and 5 to insert additional shots.

7. Click **OK** to complete the operation. The color action is added to the specification tree, as shown in Figure 2–20.

Figure 2–20

Visibility Action

How To: Control the Visibility of an Object during the Simulation

1. In the DMU Simulation toolbar, click ![icon](Visibility Action). The Edit Visibility Action dialog box opens as shown in Figure 2–21.

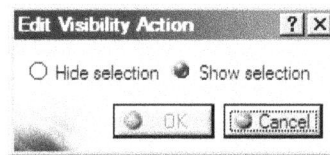

Figure 2–21

2. Select an action option.
3. Select an object. It can be a component or shuttle.
4. Click **OK** to complete the operation. The visibility action is added to the specification tree, as shown in Figure 2–22.

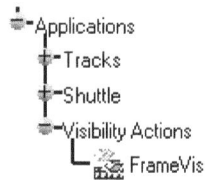

Figure 2–22

The visibility action can be renamed in the Properties dialog box.

Explode

The **Explode** tool can be used to provide offset positions for the components of an assembly before starting to create tracks. This enables you to start with an exploded assembly and simulate the assembly process.

To explode an assembly, click (Explode) in the DMU Simulation toolbar. The Explode dialog box opens as shown in Figure 2–23.

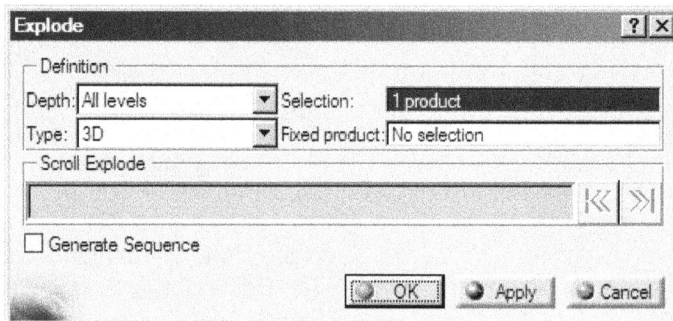

Figure 2–23

Make the appropriate selections and click **Apply** to explode the assembly.

Practice 2a

Fitting Actions

Practice Objectives

- Create a track, a color action, and a visibility action.
- Modify a shot in a track.
- Use the Reuse Shot tool.

In this practice, you will create several fitting actions to define the disassembly of specific components from the **Distributor** assembly shown in Figure 2–24.

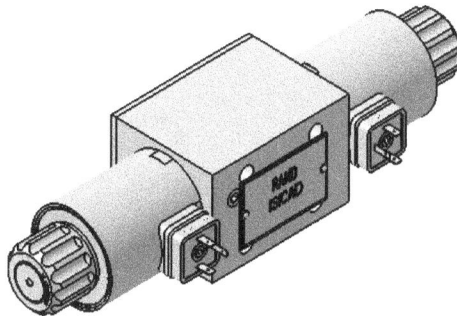

Figure 2–24

You will define tracks to move the selected components away from the assembly. You will also define color actions to help identify critical components, and visibility actions that hide components once they have been disassembled. The completed assembly displays as shown in Figure 2–25.

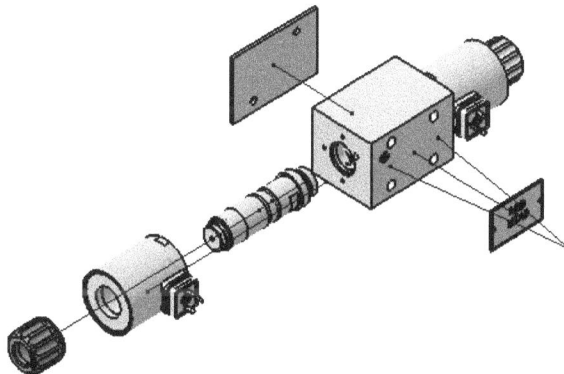

Figure 2–25

Task 1 - Open an assembly.

1. Open **Distributor_RPE3-10.CATProduct** from the *Distributor* directory. The assembly displays as shown in Figure 2–26.

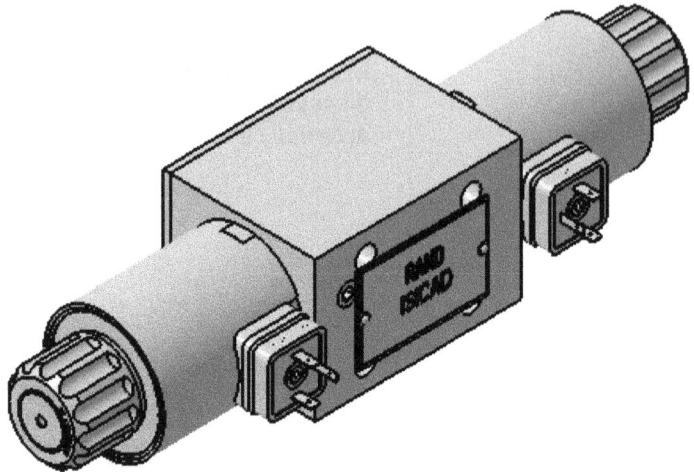

Figure 2–26

2. Investigate the assembly, which consists of many components. The bulk of the models in the assembly are symmetrical about the **Body** component. Use the **Hide/Show** function to highlight the internal components. In this practice, you will use the DMU Fitting workbench to simulate the disassembly of the components shown in Figure 2–27.

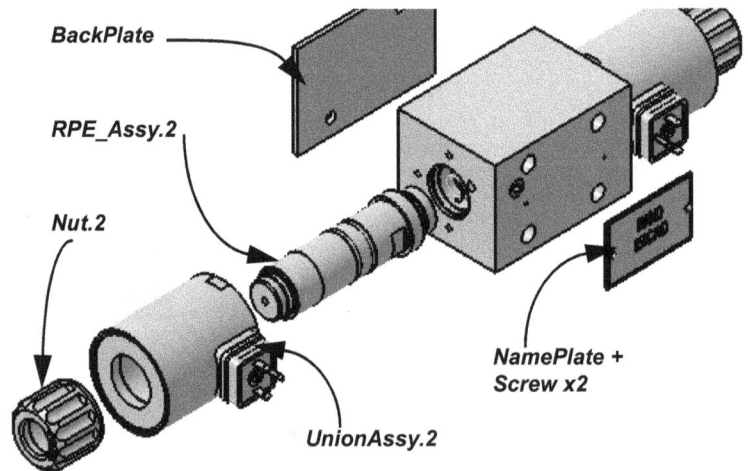

Figure 2–27

Task 2 - Create a track.

In this task, you will create a track to move the **Nut.2** component away from the assembly.

1. In the DMU Simulation toolbar, click [icon] (Track). The Track, Player, and Recorder dialog boxes open as shown in Figure 2–28.

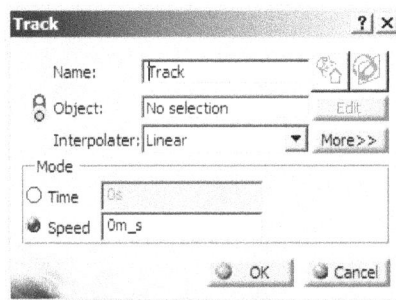

Track	? X
Name:	Track
Object:	No selection
Interpolater:	Linear

Mode
○ Time   0s
● Speed   0m_s

OK   Cancel

Figure 2–28

2. Enter the following parameters:

- *Object:* **Nut.2**
- *Name:* **Nut**
- *Interpolater:* **Linear**
- *Mode:* **Time**
- *Time:* **10s**

When an object is selected, the name for the track is entered automatically. To override this, select the object and then rename the track.

3. To move the object, select the W|Z axis and drag it to a position approximately **300mm** from the start position, as shown in Figure 2–29.

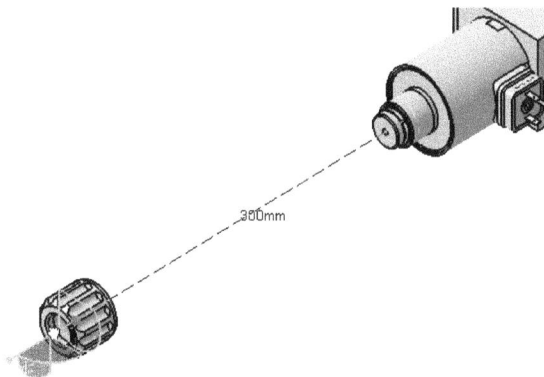

300mm

Figure 2–29

4. in the Recorder toolbar, click (Record Insert) to insert this location as the first shot of the track. The system connects the start and end positions with a line and increments the time in the Player toolbar to **10s**, as shown in Figure 2–30.

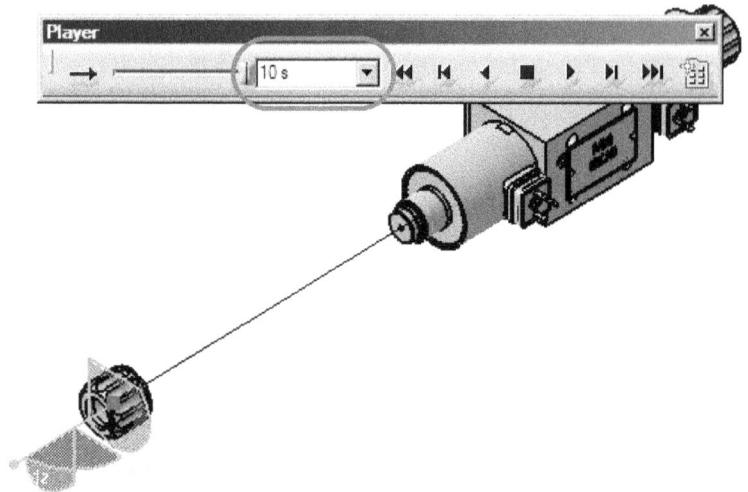

Figure 2–30

5. Click **OK** to complete the creation of the track. In the specification tree, the new track is added to the Applications branch as shown in Figure 2–31.

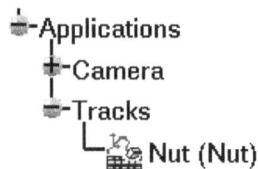

Figure 2–31

Task 3 - Replay the track.

In this task, you will use the Player toolbar to review the track that you just created.

1. Modify the track using one of the following methods:

    • In the specification tree, in the **Applications>Tracks** branch, double-click on **Nut**.

- Double-click the line that joins that start and end points of the track.

The Track dialog box and the Recorder, Player, and Manipulation toolbars open.

2. In the Player toolbar, click [⏮] (Skip to Begin) to return the shuttle to the beginning of the track.

3. Click [▶] (Play Forward). The system plays the track as it moves along the defined path.

4. Click [→] (Change Loop Mode) two times to change the Loop mode to [↺] (Continuous Loop - Reverse).

5. Replay the track. The system repeats the assembly and disassembly process.

6. Stop the playback and click [▦] (Parameters). The Player Parameters dialog box opens as shown in Figure 2–32.

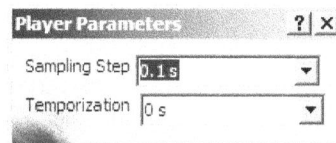

Figure 2–32

7. For the *Sampling Step*, enter **1s**.

8. Restart the playback. The system now displays 10 frames of the track instead of the default 100 frames and the resulting playback is faster.

9. For the *Sampling Step*, enter **2s** to speed up the playback.

10. Stop the replay and move the playback to the end.

11. Restore the *Sampling Step* to **1s** and the *Loop mode* to [→] (Single Loop).

12. Click **OK** to close the Track dialog box and its associated toolbars.

Task 4 - Create additional tracks.

In this task, you will create tracks for the **UnionAssy**, **RPE_Assy**, **BackPlate**, and **NamePlate** components.

1. Create a track named **UnionAssy** to move the **UnionAssy.2** component **225mm** along the W|Z axis over seven seconds. Remember to record (insert) the shot before completing the track creation. The assembly displays as shown in Figure 2–33.

*Select the **UnionAssy.2** component in the specification tree to ensure that all of its components are moved using the track.*

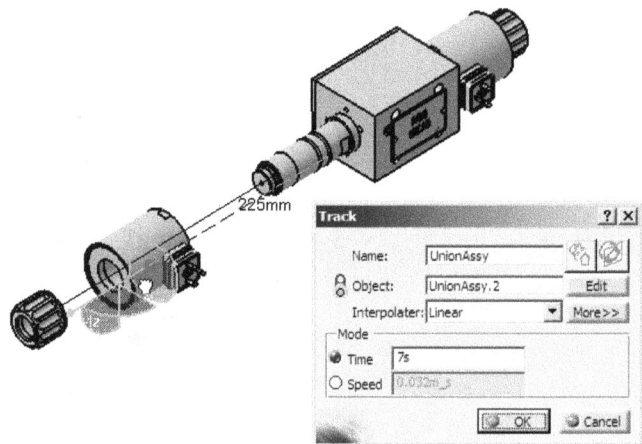

Figure 2–33

2. Create a third track named **RPE** to move the **RPE_Assy.2** component **75mm** along the W|Z axis over four seconds.

3. Create a track named **BackPlate** to move the **BackPlate** component **100mm** over five seconds, as shown in Figure 2–34.

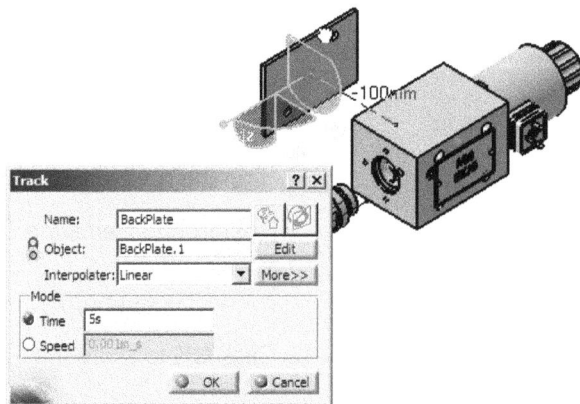

Figure 2–34

4. Create a fifth track named **NamePlate** to move the **NamePlate** component by **200mm** over five seconds in the direction shown in Figure 2–35.

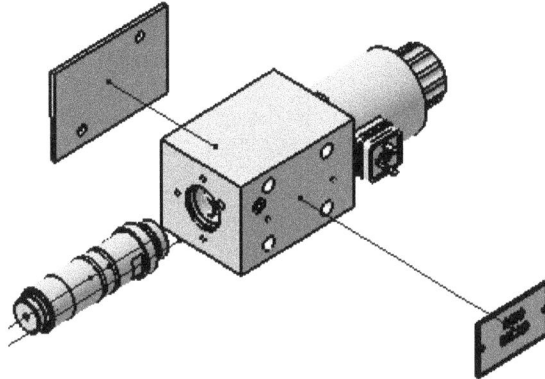

Figure 2–35

Task 5 - Create a color action.

In this task, you will create a color action to highlight the first component to be moved in the simulation. The **Nut** component will change color from yellow to orange to red.

5. In the DMU Simulation toolbar, click (Color Action). The Color Action dialog box opens as shown in Figure 2–36.

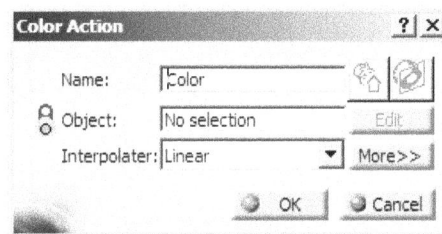

Figure 2–36

6. Make the following selections:

- *Name:* **NutColor**
- *Object:* **Nut.2**
- *Interpolater:* **Linear**

7. Once the object is selected, the Graphic Properties toolbar should open. In the Color drop-down list, select **yellow** as shown in Figure 2–37.

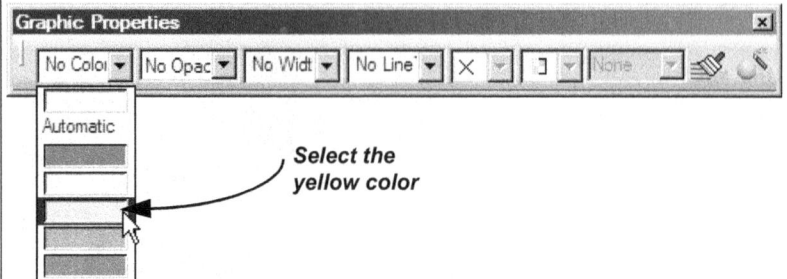

Select the
yellow color

Figure 2–37

8. In the Recorder toolbar, click (Record Insert) to insert a shot.

9. In the Color drop-down list, select **orange** and insert a shot.

10. In the Color drop-down list, select **red** and insert a shot.

11. Use the Player toolbar to replay the color action.

12. Click **OK** to complete the creation of the color action. The action displays in the specification tree, as shown in Figure 2–38.

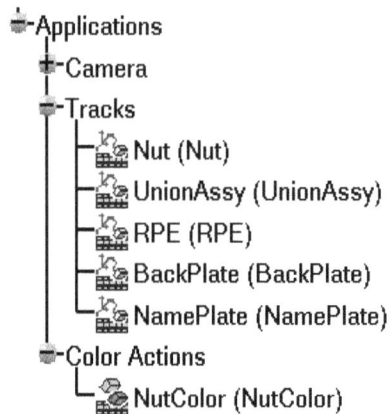

Figure 2–38

Task 6 - Create a visibility action.

When showing the assembly or disassembly of components, it is useful to hide the component when it is not attached to the assembly or being moved. In this task, you will create a visibility action to control the display of the **UnionAssy** component.

1. In the DMU Simulation toolbar, expand the Other actions

   flyout, and click (Visibility Action). The Edit Visibility Action dialog box opens as shown in Figure 2–39.

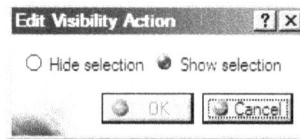

Figure 2–39

2. Select **Hide selection**.

3. In the specification tree, select the **UnionAssy.2** component.

4. Click **OK** to complete the operation. The visibility action is added to the specification tree, as shown in Figure 2–40.

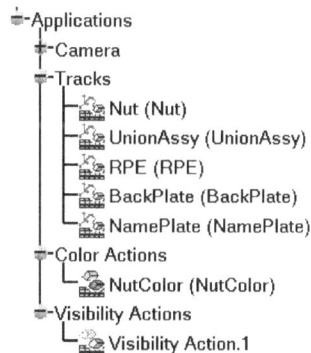

Figure 2–40

5. In the Properties dialog box, rename **Visibility Action.1** as **UnionAssyVis**.

6. Save the assembly.

Task 7 - Define tracks for the screw components.

In this task, you will create two tracks for the **Screw** components. These tracks use the position defined during the creation of the **NamePlate** track.

1. Click ▨ (Track) and select **Screw.1** as the object.

2. In the Recorder toolbar, click ▨ (Reuse Shot).

3. The system prompts you to select a track. In the model or specification tree, select the **NamePlate** track. The Reuse Shot dialog box opens as shown in Figure 2–41.

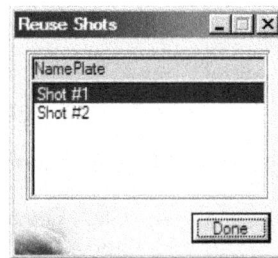

Figure 2–41

4. Select **Shot #2** and click **Done**. The system positions the screw at the exact position of the compass for the creation of Shot #2 in the **NamePlate** track.

Design Considerations

When reusing a shot from a previously created track, the system does not perform the movements that were performed to create the existing shot. Instead, the system lines up the origins of the components.

5. Click ▨ (Record Insert) to insert a shot. The track displays as shown in Figure 2–42.

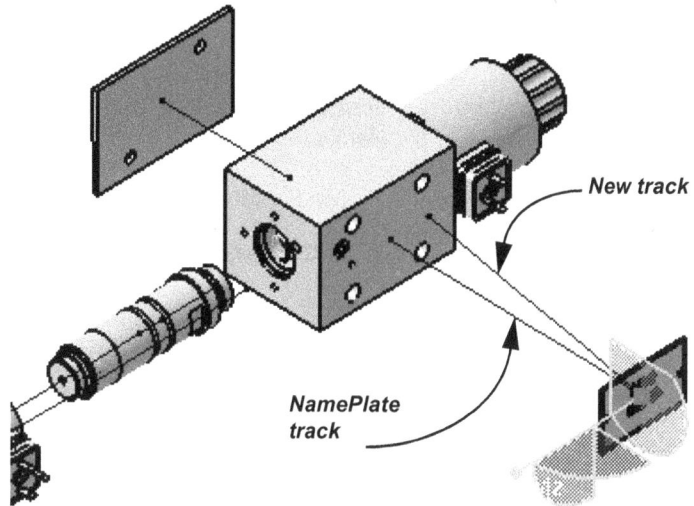

Figure 2–42

6. Enter the following parameters for the track:

   - *Name:* **Screw1**
   - *Mode:* **Time**
   - *Time:* **5s**

7. Create another track named **Screw2** that moves **Screw.2** to the Shot #2 position of **NamePlate** over five seconds. The model displays as shown in Figure 2–43.

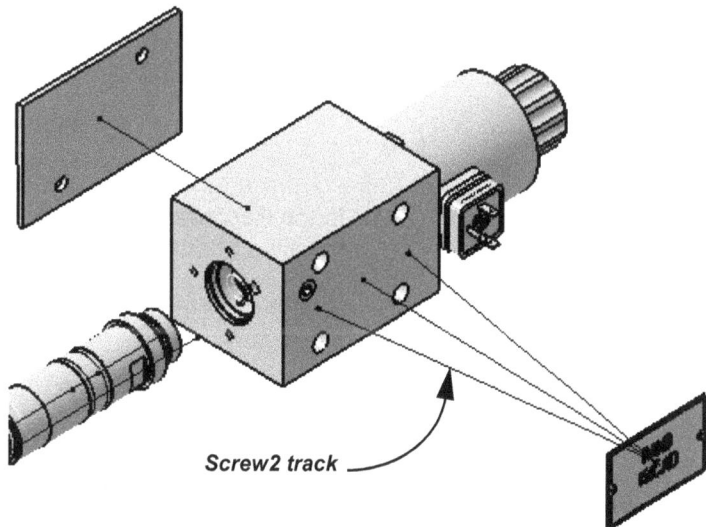

Figure 2–43

Task 8 - Modify a shot in a track.

In this task, you will modify the Shot #2 position of the **NamePlate** track so that it does not clash with the two screw tracks.

1. Modify the **NamePlate** track.

2. In the Player toolbar, select **Shot** as shown in Figure 2–44.

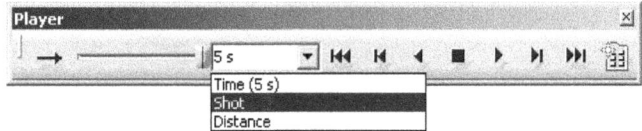

Figure 2–44

3. Ensure that the track is currently in the Shot #2 position and use the compass to drag the component back toward the assembly by approximately **70mm**, as shown in Figure 2–45.

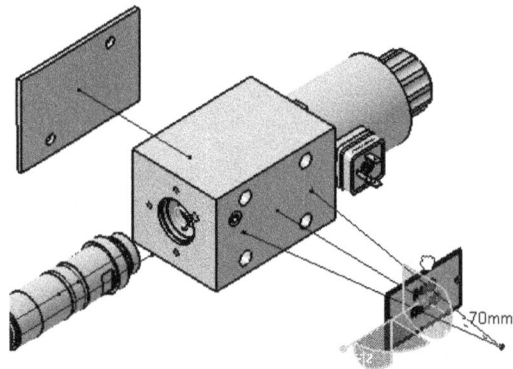

Figure 2–45

4. In the Recorder toolbar, click ![Modify] (Modify). The system modifies Shot #2 to use the current position.

5. Replay the track to confirm that the modification has taken place.

6. Click **OK** to complete the modification.

7. Save the assembly and close the window.

Design Considerations

At this point, all tracks for the simulation have been created. The next step is to add them to a sequence that enables you to replay the entire simulation.

Practice 2b | Piping Assembly

Practice Objectives

- Create a shuttle.
- Use the compass for precise positioning in a track.
- Use the Reverse Time track option.

In this practice, you will define the fitting actions for the assembly of a **By-pass Valve** arrangement into a piping assembly. The tracks that are created in this practice will use precise positioning through the use of the compass. To define the assembly of components when starting with a fully assembled model, the **Reverse Time** track option is used.

The first track to be created disassembles the entire by-pass valve arrangement. A shuttle is created to move multiple objects using a track. The completed assembly displays as shown in Figure 2–46.

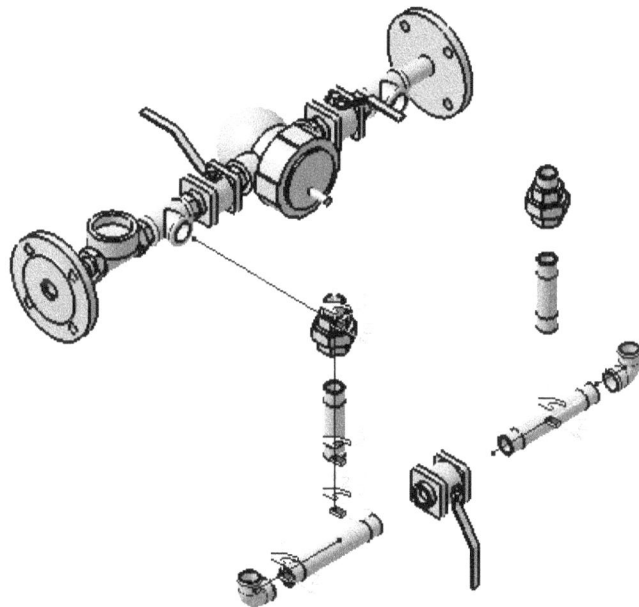

Figure 2–46

Task 1 - Open an assembly model.

1. Open **Piping.CATProduct** from the *Piping* directory. The assembly displays as shown in Figure 2–47.

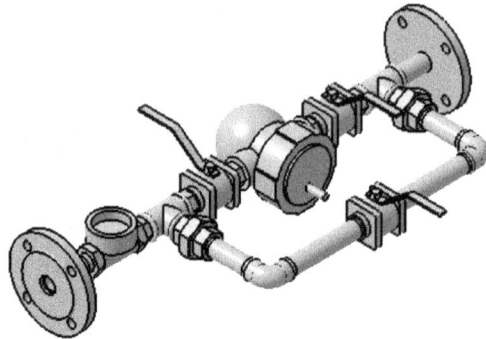

Figure 2–47

2. Investigate the assembly. The model consists of several **Flange**, **Connector**, **Valve**, and **Pipe** components. You will focus on the **By-pass Valve** arrangement that is highlighted in Figure 2–48.

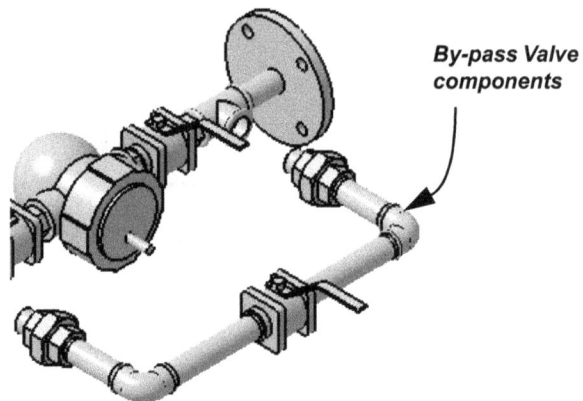

By-pass Valve components

Figure 2–48

Task 2 - Create a shuttle.

To move the **By-pass Valve** components away from the assembly, you must create a shuttle to group the components.

1. In the DMU Simulation toolbar, click (Shuttle). The Edit Shuttle dialog box and Preview window open as shown in Figure 2–49.

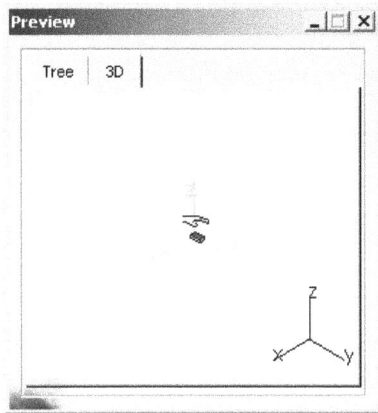

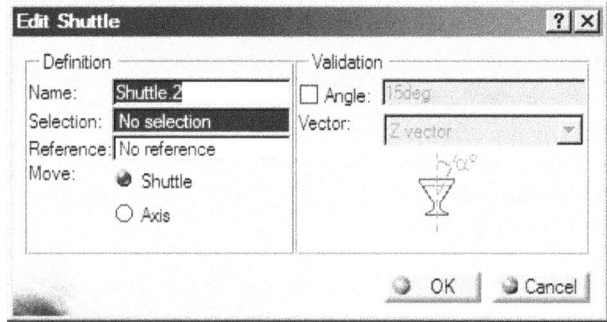

Figure 2–49

2. Rename the shuttle as **ByPass**.

3. In the specification tree, select the following components:

   - **Coupling** (2 instances)
   - **Pipe** (2 instances)
   - **Elbow** (2 instances)
   - **PipeL** (2 instances)
   - **BallValve.3**

   Once the components have been added to the shuttle, the Preview window opens as shown in Figure 2–50.

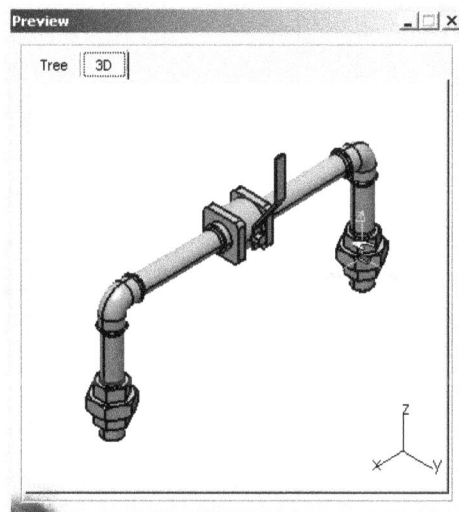

Figure 2–50

4. Accept the default options in the Edit Shuttle dialog box and click **OK** to create the shuttle. A Shuttle branch is added to the specification tree, as shown in Figure 2–51.

Figure 2–51

If the shuttle name does not automatically display, try collapsing and expanding the Shuttle branch in the specification tree.

Task 3 - Create a track.

In this task, you will create a track to move the **ByPass** shuttle away from the assembly.

1. In the DMU Simulation toolbar, click (Track). The Track dialog box (shown in Figure 2–52) and Player and Recorder toolbars open.

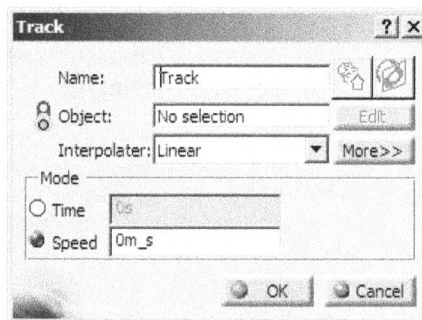

Figure 2–52

2. Enter the following parameters:

It is recommended that you select the shuttle object before entering a name. The selection of the object enters a default value in the Name field.

- *Object:* select the **ByPass shuttle** in the specification tree
- *Name:* **ByPass Assy**
- *Interpolater:* **Linear**
- *Mode:* **Time**
- *Time:* **10s**

3. To move the shuttle, select the W|Z axis and drag it to a position approximately **250mm** from the start position, as shown in Figure 2–53.

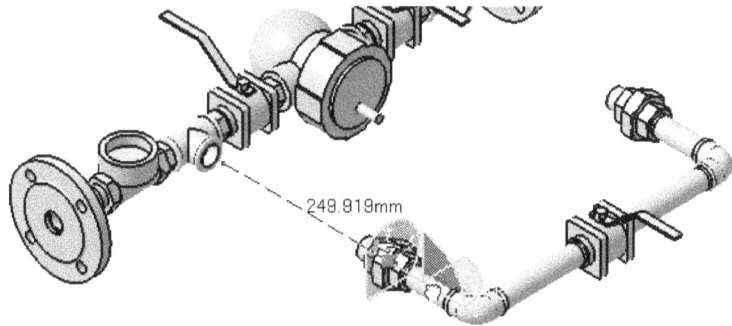

Figure 2–53

4. This position is the first shot of the track. In the Recorder toolbar, click ⊞ (Record Insert). The Player toolbar updates to display the current time as **10s**.

Design Considerations

When dragging objects during the creation of a track, the location is approximate. To specify the exact positioning, you must edit the compass using the Parameters for Compass Manipulation dialog box. This enables you to enter coordinates or increments for the position and orientation of the object.

In the next step, you will rotate the shuttle by exactly 90 degrees using ⊞ (Editor) in the Manipulation toolbar.

5. Click ⊞ (Editor). The Parameters for Compass Manipulation dialog box opens as shown in Figure 2–54.

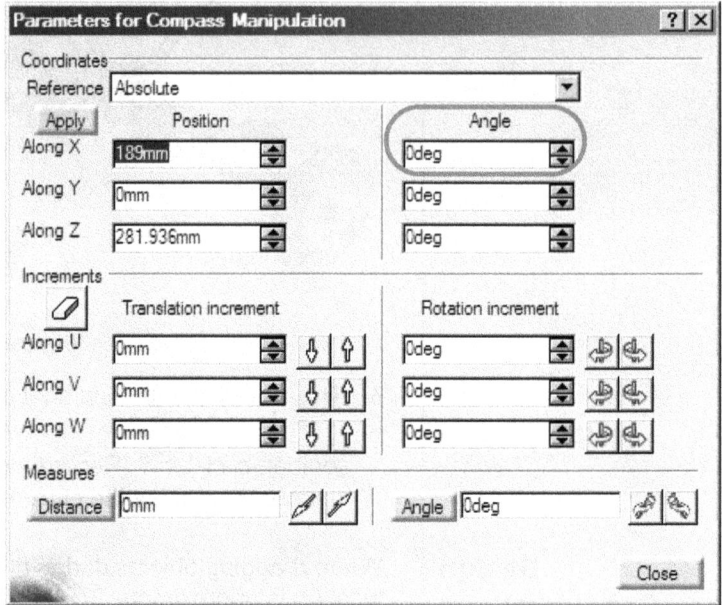

Figure 2–54

6. In the *Angle* field for the Along X direction, enter **90** and click **Apply**. The shuttle rotates as shown in Figure 2–55.

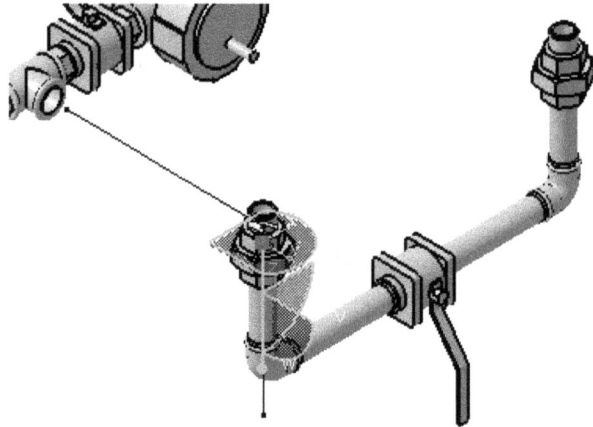

Figure 2–55

7. Click ⊞ (Record Insert) to insert the new orientation as the next shot.

8. Close the Parameters for Compass Manipulation dialog box.

9. For the last shot, drag the object along the W|Z axis by approximately **200mm** and click ⊞ (Record Insert).

10. Click **OK** to complete the creation of the **ByPass Assy** track.

Task 4 - Move the Coupling and Pipe components.

In this task, you will create two shuttles and two tracks to move the **Coupling** and **Pipe** components to the positions shown in Figure 2–56. A shuttle is used to ensure that the left and right parts are translated by the same distance.

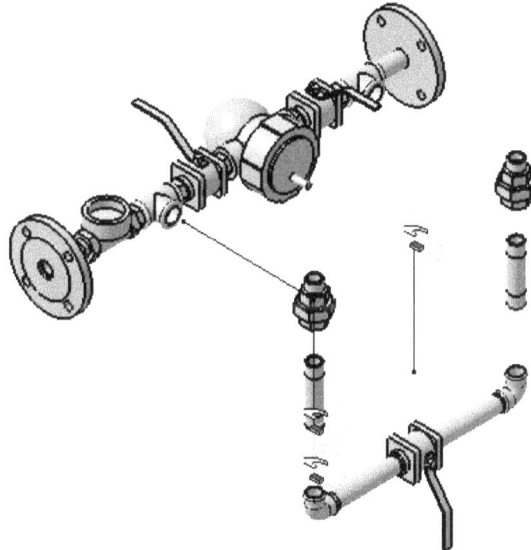

Figure 2–56

1. Create a shuttle named **Couple + Pipe** and add the two coupling components and two pipe components. The Preview window opens as shown in Figure 2–57.

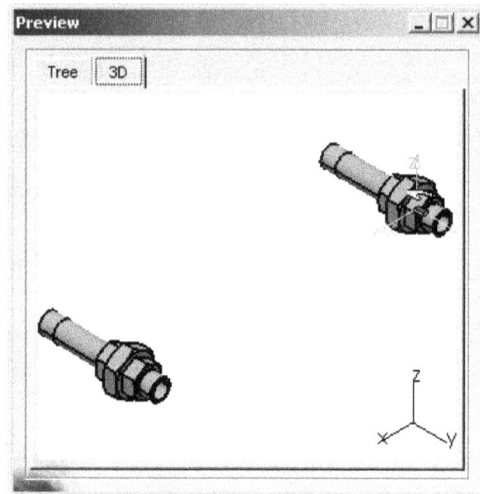

Figure 2–57

2. Create a track named **Couple + Pipe** to move the **Couple + Pipe** shuttle upwards by approximately **200mm** over five seconds, as shown in Figure 2–58. Be sure to click (Record Insert) before completing the creation of the track.

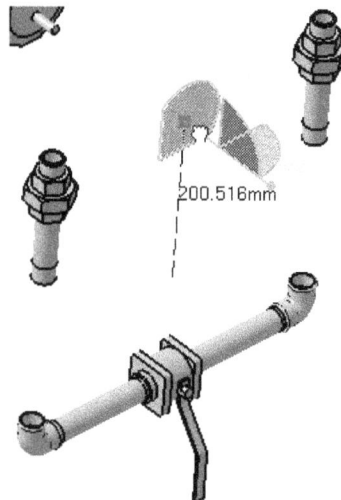

Figure 2–58

3. Create a shuttle named **Pipe** and add the two **Pipe** components. The Preview window opens as shown in Figure 2–59.

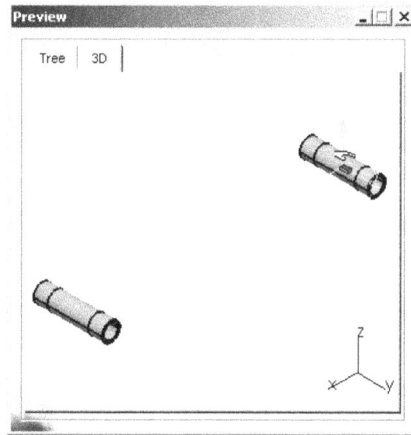

Figure 2–59

4. Create another track named **Pipe** to move the **Pipe** shuttle downwards by approximately **75mm** over three seconds.

Task 5 - Move the Elbow and PipeL components.

In this task, you will move the left and right **Elbow** and **PipeL** components. They will move in opposite directions, so a single shuttle cannot be used. To ensure that they are translated by identical distances, the Editor is used to enter the exact translations.

1. Create a shuttle named **Left hand** and add **Elbow.1** and **PipeL.1**.

2. Create another shuttle named **Right hand** and add **Elbow.2** and **PipeL.2**.

3. Create a track named **Left** and select the **Left hand** shuttle.

4. Select **Time** and enter **3s**.

5. In the Manipulation toolbar, click ⊞ (Editor). In the *Translation increment* field for Along U, enter **100**.

6. Click ⊞ to move the object to the left side by **100mm**.

7. Close the Parameters for Compass Manipulation dialog box.

8. Click (Record Insert) to insert a shot.

9. Complete the creation of the track.

10. Create a second track named **Right** and select the **Right hand** shuttle.

11. Use Steps 5 to 9 to move the shuttle **100mm** to the right over three seconds, as shown in Figure 2–60.

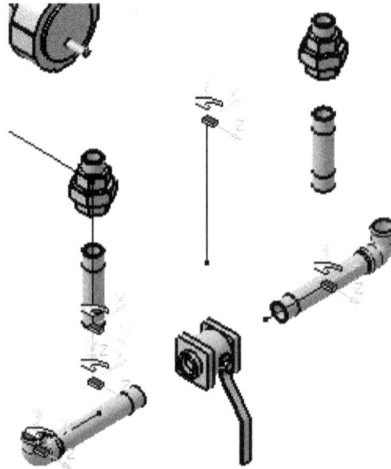

Figure 2–60

12. Create another track named **ElbowL** to move **Elbow.1 50mm** to the left over three seconds. You can either change the *Along U* value in the Editor dialog box to **50mm**, or set the value to **0mm** and drag the compass.

13. Create a final track named **ElbowR** to move **Elbow.2 50mm** to the right over three seconds.

Task 6 - Apply reverse time to the tracks.

In this task, you will use the **Reverse Time** option so that all of the tracks are played backwards. This enables you to simulate the assembly process of the **By-pass Valve** assembly.

Alternatively, you can select the first track in the specification tree, hold <Shift>, and select the last track.

1. Hold <Ctrl> and select all of the tracks in the specification tree.

2. Right-click on the selection and select **Selected objects> Reverse time**. A Reverse time branch is added beneath each track, as shown in Figure 2–61.

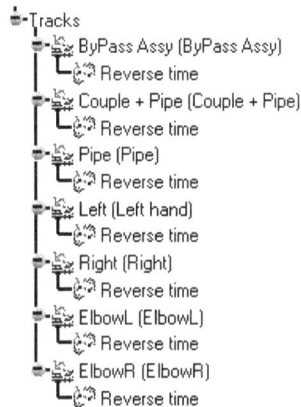

Figure 2–61

Task 7 - Replay the ByPass Assy track.

1. In the specification tree, double-click on the **ByPass Assy** track.

2. Use the Player toolbar to return the track to its start position. The track now starts with the shuttle in its disassembled position.

3. Play the track. It simulates the shuttle being assembled into the product.

4. Close the Track dialog box.

5. Save the assembly and close the window.

Sequencing

In this chapter, you will learn how to arrange tracks, color actions, visibility actions, and previously created sequences using Sequences.

Learning Objectives in this Chapter

- Generate a Sequence to arrange tracks, color actions, visibility actions, and previously created sequences.
- Use the Gantt Chart to create and generate a sequence.
- Create a Replay to compile a simulation so that it can be reviewed.
- Generate a Video to review a simulation outside CATIA or ENOVIA.

3.1 Generate a Sequence

A sequence is a recording tool that enables you to arrange tracks, color actions, visibility actions, and previously created sequences. The timing of the sequence objects can be controlled and pauses and delays can be inserted to create the required effect. This arrangement can be replayed to review the entire fitting simulation.

General Steps

Use the following general steps to create a sequence:

1. Start the creation of a sequence.
2. Insert the action(s) into the sequence.
3. Organize the actions in the sequence.
4. Validate the sequence.

Step 1 - Start the creation of a sequence.

Click ⬛ (Edit Sequence) in the DMU Simulation toolbar. The Edit Sequence dialog box opens as shown in Figure 3–1. All fitting actions and previously created sequences are listed in the left column. The right column displays the actions that have been added to the sequence.

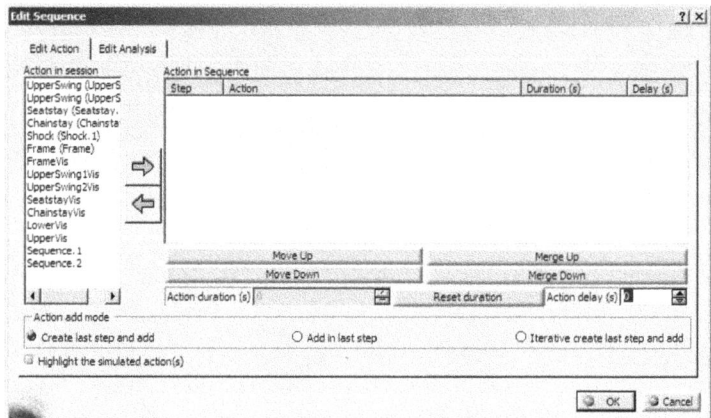

Figure 3–1

Step 2 - Insert the action(s) into the sequence.

The sequence consists of a series of steps. Each step can contain any number of actions that are performed simultaneously before moving onto the next step.

How To: Insert an Action into the Sequence

1. In the *Action add mode* field, select an option. The options are described as follows:

Option	Description
Create last step and add	Adds the selected actions as a new step at the end of the sequence. This is the default option.
Add in last step	Merges the selected action(s) into the last step of the sequence.
Iterative create last step and add	Adds the selected actions as unique steps in the sequence. For example, if three actions are selected the system creates three new steps at the end of the sequence. The system organizes the new steps in the order in which the actions display in the *Action in session* column.

2. In the *Action in session* column, select the action(s). Multiple actions can be selected using <Ctrl>.

3. Click ⇨ to add the selected action(s) to the sequence. For example, the **Frame**, **Shock**, and **Chainstay** actions were added using the **Iterative create last step and add** option, as shown in Figure 3–2.

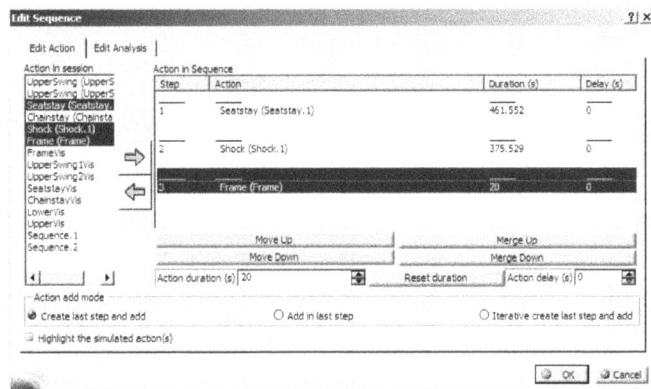

Figure 3–2

Continue adding actions until all of the required actions display in the *Actions in Sequence* column.

Step 3 - Organize the actions in the sequence.

Although you can control the placement of actions in the sequence using the **Action add mode** options, you might want to further reorganize the position of the actions. The four buttons used to organize the actions in a sequence are described in the table below. All of the operations are performed on the **Shock** action in the sequence shown in Figure 3–3.

Action in Sequence			
Step	Action	Duration (s)	Delay (s)
1	Seatstay (Seatstay.1)	461.552	0
2	Shock (Shock.1)	375.529	0
3	Frame (Frame)	20	0

Move Up	Merge Up
Move Down	Merge Down

Figure 3–3

Button	Example
Move Up	<table><tr><th>Step</th><th>Action</th></tr><tr><td>1</td><td>Shock (Shock.1)</td></tr><tr><td>2</td><td>Seatstay (Seatstay.1)</td></tr><tr><td>3</td><td>Frame (Frame)</td></tr></table>
Move Down	<table><tr><th>Step</th><th>Action</th></tr><tr><td>1</td><td>Seatstay (Seatstay.1)</td></tr><tr><td>2</td><td>Frame (Frame)</td></tr><tr><td>3</td><td>Shock (Shock.1)</td></tr></table>

Merge Up

Step	Action
1	Seatstay (Seatstay.1)
1	**Shock (Shock.1)**
2	Frame (Frame)

Merge Down

Step	Action
1	Seatstay (Seatstay.1)
2	Frame (Frame)
2	**Shock (Shock.1)**

Duration & Delay

The duration of each action can also be controlled using the *Action duration* field. Enter a time in seconds for the duration of the selected action. A delay can also be added to the action. The action is not played in the sequence until the time in seconds entered into the *Action delay* field has elapsed.

Step 4 - Validate the sequence.

Once all of the actions have been inserted and organized, the sequence can be validated by playing it from beginning to end using the Player toolbar. If the sequence replays correctly, complete the creation of the sequence by clicking **OK**. The new sequence is added to the **Applications>Sequence** branch in the specification tree, as shown in Figure 3–4. The sequence can be renamed in the Properties dialog box.

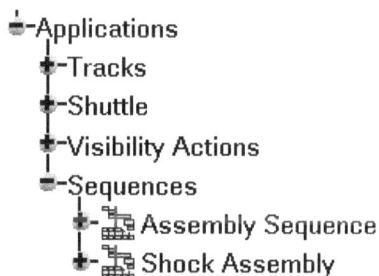

```
-Applications
    -Tracks
    -Shuttle
    -Visibility Actions
    -Sequences
        - Assembly Sequence
        - Shock Assembly
```

Figure 3–4

3.2 Use the Gantt Chart

The Gantt Chart is another method of creating and arranging a sequence. The chart provides a visual display of the order and duration of the actions added to an existing sequence. The duration and start and end times of each action can be dynamically modified using the chart. The modifications made to the Gantt Chart are associative to the Sequence Editor.

General Steps

Use the following general steps to edit a sequence using a Gantt Chart:

1. Select the sequence to be modified.
2. Open the Gantt Chart window.
3. Modify the parameters of the actions.

Step 1 - Select the sequence to be modified.

Since the Gantt Chart is only displaying information about a previously created sequence, you must first select the sequence to be modified or reviewed in the specification tree.

Step 2 - Open the Gantt Chart window.

Select **Window>New Gantt Chart Window**. The sequence displays in a new window displayed in a gantt chart format, as shown in Figure 3–5. The left side of the window only lists the fitting actions that have been added to the sequence, and their duration and beginning and ending times. The right side of the window displays a graphical representation of the sequence.

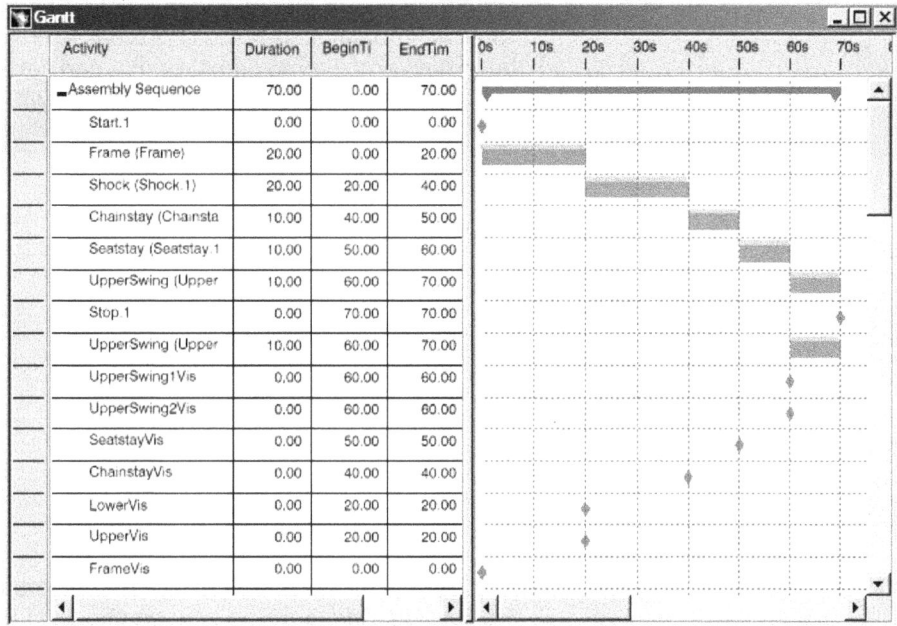

Figure 3–5

Step 3 - Modify the parameters of the actions.

The duration and beginning and ending times of an action can be modified in two ways:

1. Double-click on the appropriate value in the left side of the window. A dialog box opens, enabling you to enter a new value as shown in Figure 3–6. This method is useful when you need to specify exact values for the duration and beginning and ending times.

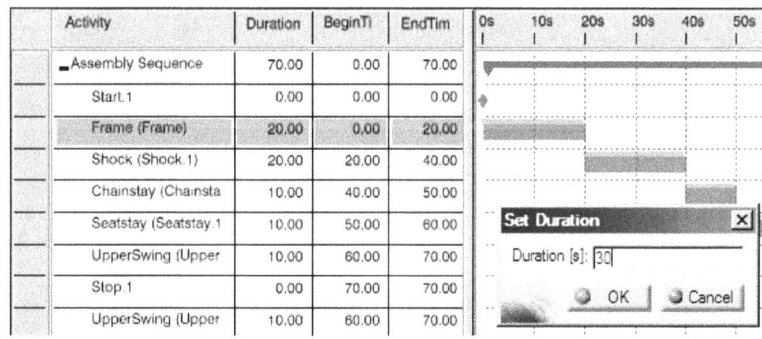

Figure 3–6

2. Drag the bars for the appropriate action on the left side of the window. You can select the entire bar to change the beginning and ending times, or you can select the end of the bar (so that an arrow displays, as shown in Figure 3–7) to change the duration. A change in duration updates all of the downstream actions.

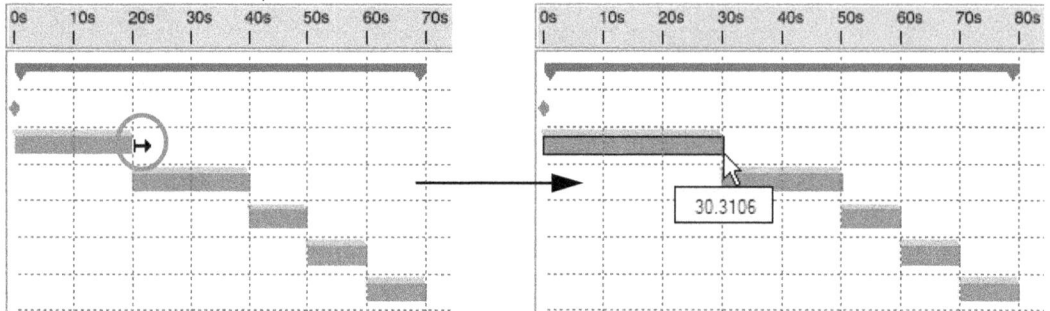

Figure 3–7

Any changes to the Gantt Chart are automatically updated in the Edit Sequence dialog box, as shown in Figure 3–8. The Gantt Chart window can be closed at any time without requiring a save operation.

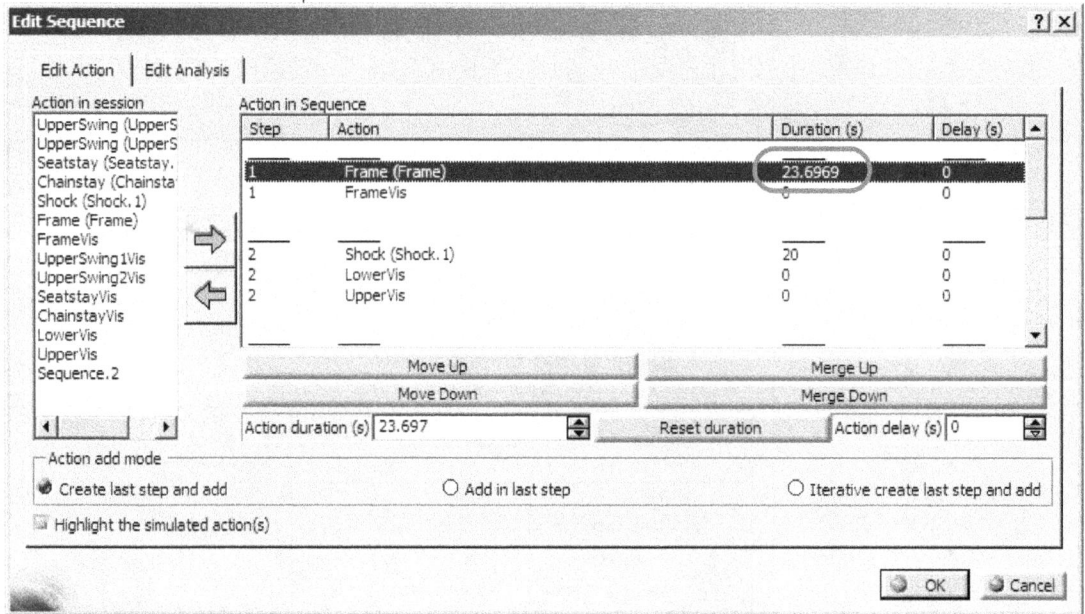

Figure 3–8

3.3 Create a Replay

A replay compiles a simulation so that it can be reviewed. Since the simulation has been compiled, the system does not need to perform any geometry calculations during the review. Therefore, a replay typically runs faster than a sequence.

Once compiled, the replay is stored in the specification tree for easy access. The replay can be reviewed outside the DMU Fitting workbench and therefore does not require a DMU Fitting license to be played. The replay is only accessible in CATIA or ENOVIA DMU.

How To: Create a Replay

1. In the specification tree, select a sequence to be compiled.
2. Select **Tools>Simulation>Generate Replay**. The Replay Generation dialog box opens as shown in Figure 3–9. Additionally, the Player toolbar opens and enables you to review the simulation you are about to compile.

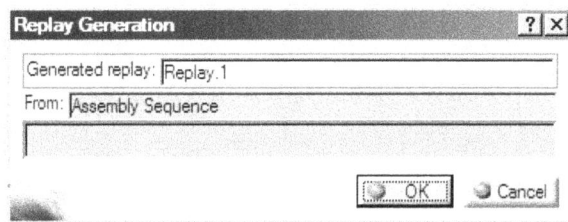

Figure 3–9

3. In the *Generated replay* field, enter a name for the replay.
4. Click **OK**. The system compiles the replay and adds it to the specification tree as shown in Figure 3–10.

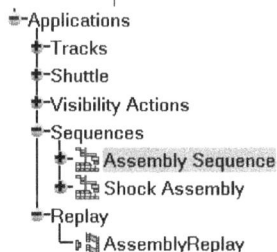

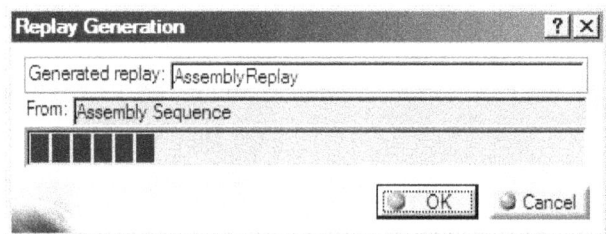

Figure 3–10

5. In the specification tree, double-click on the replay to open the Player toolbar and review the replay.

3.4 Generate a Video

Generating video enables you to review a simulation outside CATIA or ENOVIA. The system generates a file that can be played in Windows Media Player or another multimedia tool.

How To: Generate a Video File

1. In the specification tree, select a sequence or replay to be converted to video.
2. Select **Tools>Simulation>Generate Video**. The Video Generation dialog box opens as shown in Figure 3–11. Additionally, the Player toolbar opens and enables you to review the simulation you are about to compile.

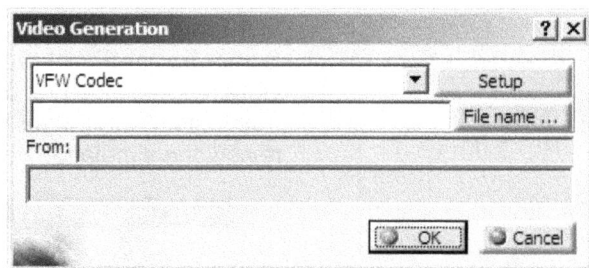

Figure 3–11

3. In the drop-down list, select an option to define the type of video output. Three types of animation files are available:

   • **VFW Codec:** Generates an AVI standard format that can be viewed in most Windows Media players.

   • **DirectShow Filter:** Generates an MPG standard format that can be viewed in most Windows Media players. MPG offers higher compression, resulting in a smaller file size than AVI.

   • **Still Image Capture:** Generates an animation that is viewable in all operating systems. Consists of a group of a series of JPEG screen captures.

4. Click **File name** and enter a filename and location in which to save the video file.

5. Click **Setup** to configure the animation file. The Choose Compressor dialog box opens as shown in Figure 3–12.

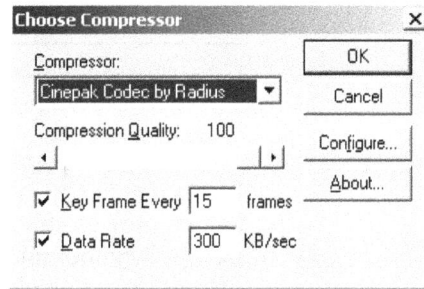

Figure 3–12

The dialog box can be used for the following purposes:

- Select the compressor (or codec) used to compress the file.

- Specify the compression quality.

- Select **Color** or **Black and White** output using **Configure**.

6. Click **OK** to create the video. The simulation plays while it is recorded to the video file. Once complete, the file can be retrieved from the specified directory.

Practice 3a

Distributor Sequence

Practice Objectives

- Create a sequence.
- Reorder and merge fitting actions in a sequence.
- Generate a replay from a sequence.

In this practice, you will define the disassembly sequence for the **Distributor** assembly. The sequence brings all of the fitting actions together (including tracks, visibility actions, and color actions) into a single simulation that can be reviewed. Once the sequence is created, you will save it as a replay that can be accessed from anywhere in the CATIA and ENOVIA DMU interface.

Task 1 - Open an assembly.

1. Open **Distributor_RPE3-10.CATProduct** from the Distributor directory. The assembly displays as shown in Figure 3–13.

   If you did not complete the previous practice, open **Distributor_RPE3-10_Completed.CATProduct** in the *Distributor>Completed* directory.

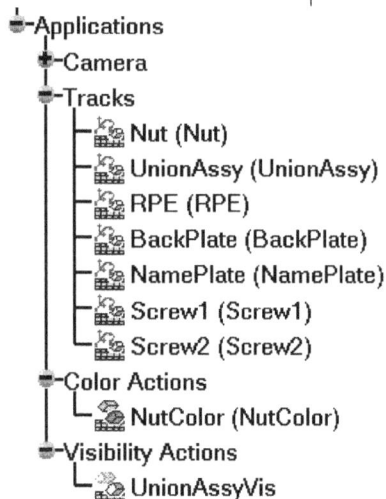

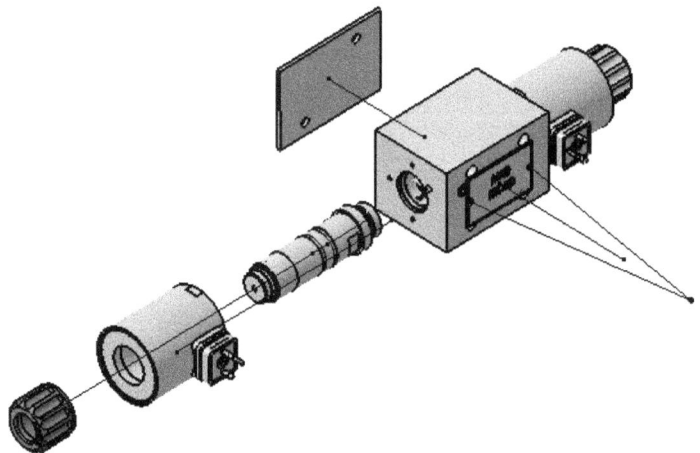

- Applications
  - Camera
  - Tracks
    - Nut (Nut)
    - UnionAssy (UnionAssy)
    - RPE (RPE)
    - BackPlate (BackPlate)
    - NamePlate (NamePlate)
    - Screw1 (Screw1)
    - Screw2 (Screw2)
  - Color Actions
    - NutColor (NutColor)
  - Visibility Actions
    - UnionAssyVis

Figure 3–13

Task 2 - Create a sequence.

In this task, you will develop a sequence. The sequence adds the fitting actions that have been created in the assembly and organizes them so that the disassembly of the distributor components can be simulated.

The order of the fitting actions in the new sequence is shown in Figure 3–14.

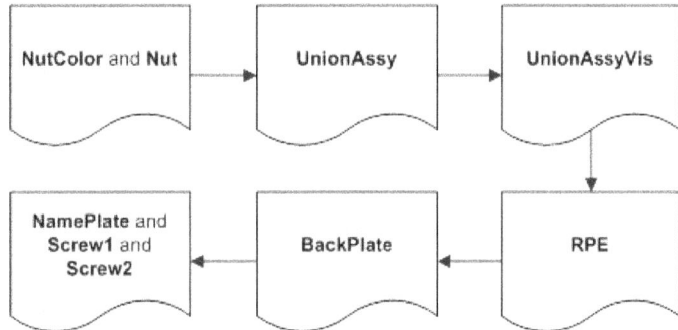

Figure 3–14

1. In the DMU Simulation toolbar, click (Edit Sequence). The Edit Sequence dialog box opens as shown in Figure 3–15. The Player toolbar also opens.

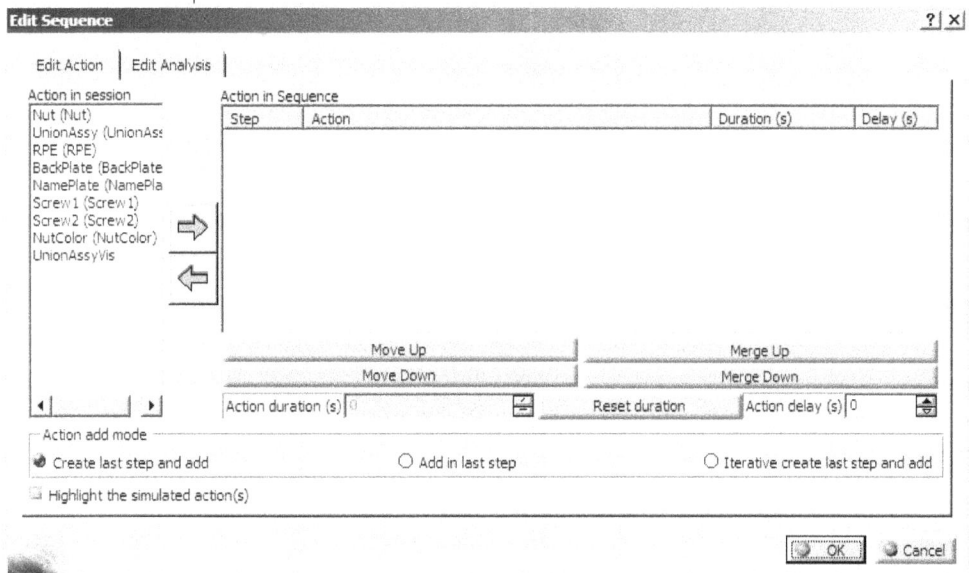

Figure 3–15

Design Considerations

The first step adds the **UnionAssy** and **UnionAssyVis** actions. These actions are added to the same step, so the **Create last step and add** option should be used.

2. In the *Action add mode* field, ensure that the **Create last step and add** option is selected.

3. In the *Action in session* column, use <Ctrl> to select **Nut** and **NutColor** and click [⇨] to add them to the Action in Sequence, as shown in Figure 3–16.

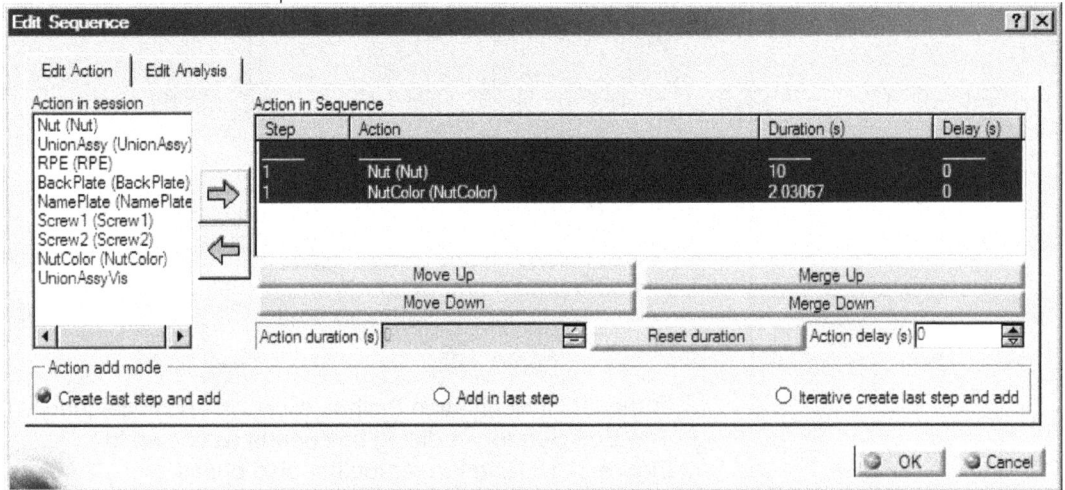

Figure 3–16

The next step is to add several actions as unique steps in the sequence. This is done using the **Iterative create last step and add** option. The system adds these actions in the order in which they display in the *Actions in session* column. Therefore, they have to be reorganized after they are added.

4. In the *Action add mode* field, select the **Iterative create last step and add** option.

5. In the *Action in session* column, select the following actions to insert into the *Action in Sequence* area:

- **UnionAssy**
- **RPE**
- **BackPlate**
- **UnionAssyVis**

The system adds each fitting action as a new step in the sequence, as shown in Figure 3–17.

Action in Sequence

Step	Action	Duration (s)	Delay (s)
1	Nut (Nut)	10	0
1	NutColor (NutColor)	2.03067	0
2	UnionAssy (UnionAssy)	7	0
3	RPE (RPE)	4	0
4	BackPlate (BackPlate)	5	0
5	UnionAssyVis	0	0

Figure 3–17

6. Use the **Move Up** and **Move Down** buttons to reorder the steps of the sequence so that they display as shown in Figure 3–18.

Action in Sequence

Step	Action	Duration (s)	Delay (s)
1	Nut (Nut)	10	0
1	NutColor (NutColor)	2.03067	0
2	UnionAssy (UnionAssy)	7	0
3	UnionAssyVis	0	0
4	RPE (RPE)	4	0
5	BackPlate (BackPlate)	5	0

Figure 3–18

7. Add the following actions as the last step in the sequence:

- **NamePlate**
- **Screw1**
- **Screw2**

If they were added using the **Iterative create last step and add** option, the **Merge Up** and **Merge Down** buttons can be used to modify the sequence so that it displays as shown in Figure 3–19.

Action in Sequence

Step	Action	Duration (s)	Delay (s)
1	Nut (Nut)	10	0
1	NutColor (NutColor)	2.03067	0
2	UnionAssy (UnionAssy)	7	0
3	UnionAssyVis	0	0
4	RPE (RPE)	4	0
5	BackPlate (BackPlate)	5	0
6	NamePlate (NamePlate)	5	0
6	Screw1 (Screw1)	5	0
6	Screw2 (Screw2)	5	0

Figure 3–19

Do not close the Sequence Editor dialog box. It is used in the next task.

Task 3 - Modify the delay and duration for actions in the sequence.

In this task, you will add a delay to the sequence so that the timing of the fitting actions matches your design intent. For example, a delay will be added to the **Nut** track so that the **NutColor** action can complete before the component is moved.

1. Select the **NutColor** action in Step #1. The *Action Duration* and *Delay* fields can now be modified.

2. In the *Action Duration* field, enter **0.5**. The color change for the **Nut** now take 0.5 seconds. You might need to select the action from the list again to update the sequence with the duration change.

3. Select the **Nut** action and enter a delay of **0.5**. The **Nut** track starts immediately after the **NutColor** action has finished. The Sequence Editor dialog box opens as shown in Figure 3–20.

Action in Sequence

Step	Action	Duration (s)	Delay (s)
1	Nut (Nut)	10	0.5
1	NutColor (NutColor)	0.5	0

Figure 3–20

4. Select the **NamePlate** and enter a *Delay* of **2**. This enables the two **Screw** tracks to get a head start before the **NamePlate** track begins.

Task 4 - Replay the sequence and perform any modifications.

Before accepting any sequence, you should always review it to verify that the settings and order fit your design intent. Changes should be made to the sequence before a replay or video.

1. Locate the Player toolbar and click ▶ to replay the sequence.

2. Adjust the sequence, if required.

3. Once the sequence definition is complete, click **OK**.

Task 5 - Create a replay.

1. In the specification tree, select **Sequence.1**.

2. Select **Tools>Simulation>Generate Replay**. The Replay Generation dialog box opens as shown in Figure 3–21.

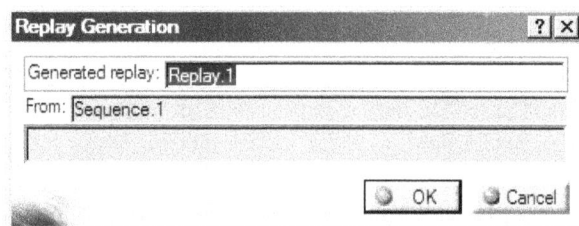

Replay Generation   ? X

Generated replay: Replay.1

From: Sequence.1

○ OK   ○ Cancel

Figure 3–21

3. Rename the *replay* as **AssemblySim**.

4. Click **OK**. The system begins to play the sequence and stores the information in a new replay, as shown in Figure 3–22.

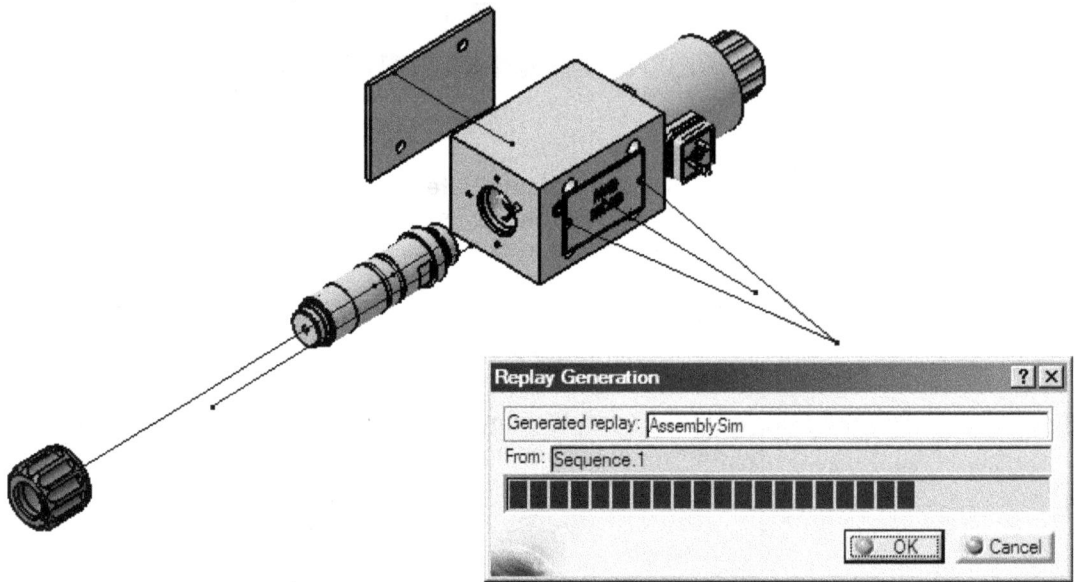

Figure 3–22

5. Once the replay is generated, the Replay Generation dialog box closes and the replay is added to the specification tree, as shown in Figure 3–23.

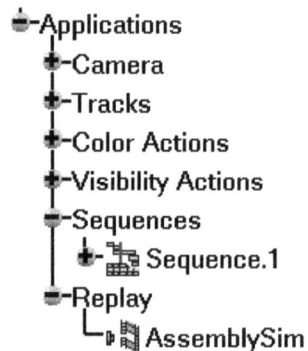

Figure 3–23

Task 6 - Review the replay.

1. In the specification tree, double-click on AssemblySim to review the replay. The Replay dialog box opens as shown in Figure 3–24.

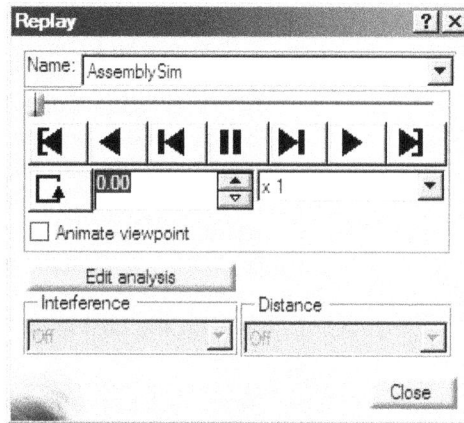

Figure 3–24

2. Click [▶] to review the simulation. The replay can be reviewed from any workbench in CATIA or ENOVIA DMU.

3. Close the Replay dialog box.

4. Save the assembly and close the window.

Practice 3b

Piping

Practice Objectives

- Create a sequence with limited instruction.
- Open a Gantt Chart window.
- Modify a sequence using a Gantt Chart.
- Generate an AVI video from a sequence.

In this practice, you will generate the assembly simulation of the **By-pass** components onto the **Piping** assembly. You will create this sequence with limited instruction to test your knowledge of sequence creation. Once the sequence has been created, you will open a Gantt Chart window and use it to modify the duration and delay of specific fitting actions. The resulting simulation is saved to a Microsoft AVI file format so that it can be viewed outside the CATIA or ENOVIA DMU products.

Task 1 - Open an assembly.

1. Open **Piping.CATProduct** from the *Piping* directory. The assembly displays as shown in Figure 3–25.

   If you did not complete Practice 2b, open **Piping_Complete.CATProduct** in the *Piping>Completed* directory.

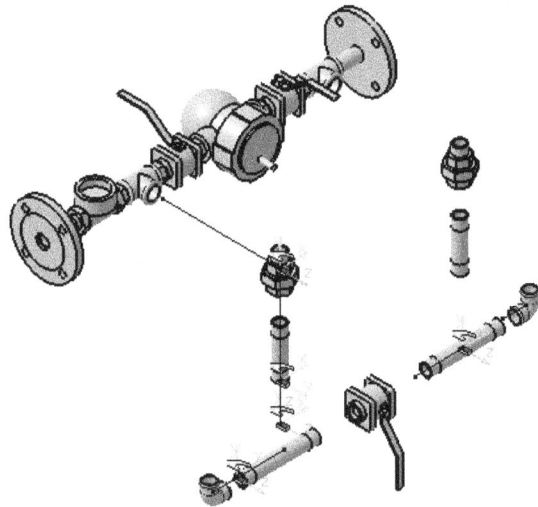

Figure 3–25

Task 2 - Create a sequence.

In this task, you will develop a sequence to bring the components of the **By-pass Valve** together, and then assemble the group of components into the **Piping** assembly. The sequence is created with limited instruction.

1. Create a sequence that simulates the assembly of the **By-pass Valve** components onto the **Piping** assembly. Use the flowchart shown in Figure 3–26 as a guide to the order in which the fitting actions should be sequenced. No durations or delays need to be specified at this time.

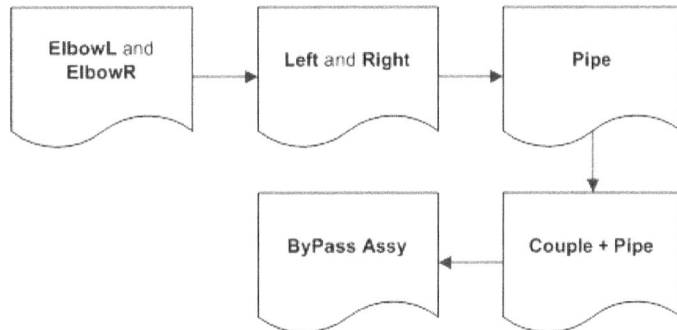

Figure 3–26

The position of some components in the sequence could vary depending on the installed CATIA Service Pack.

2. Once the sequence has been defined, use the Player toolbar to review the sequence and make any adjustments before completing the sequence creation.

3. Rename the sequence as **ByPass Assembly**.

Task 3 - Open a Gantt Chart window.

In this task, you will use the Gantt Chart view of the sequence to perform timing modifications. The Gantt Chart is a useful method of visualizing the order and timing of the fitting actions in the sequence.

1. In the specification tree, preselect the **ByPass Assembly** sequence.

2. Select **Window>New Gantt Chart Window**. A Gantt Chart of the sequence opens, as shown in Figure 3–27.

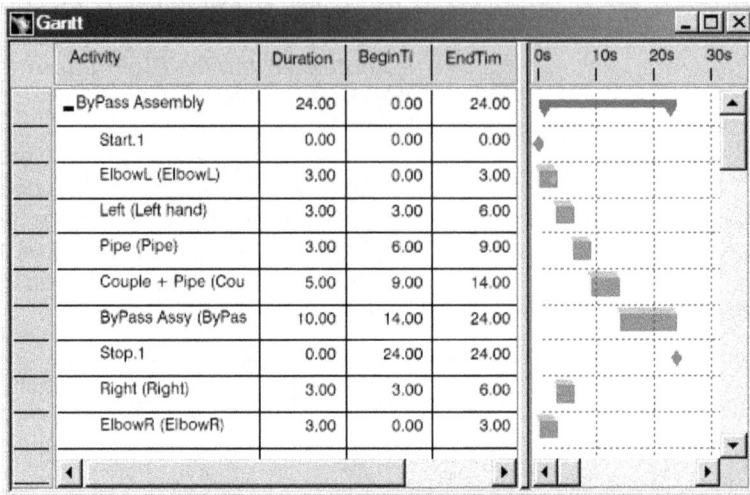

Activity	Duration	BeginTi	EndTim
ByPass Assembly	24.00	0.00	24.00
Start.1	0.00	0.00	0.00
ElbowL (ElbowL)	3.00	0.00	3.00
Left (Left hand)	3.00	3.00	6.00
Pipe (Pipe)	3.00	6.00	9.00
Couple + Pipe (Cou	5.00	9.00	14.00
ByPass Assy (ByPas	10.00	14.00	24.00
Stop.1	0.00	24.00	24.00
Right (Right)	3.00	3.00	6.00
ElbowR (ElbowR)	3.00	0.00	3.00

Figure 3–27

3. Adjust the scale of the timeline by right-clicking on the time axis labels and selecting **Set Scale Units**, as shown in Figure 3–28.

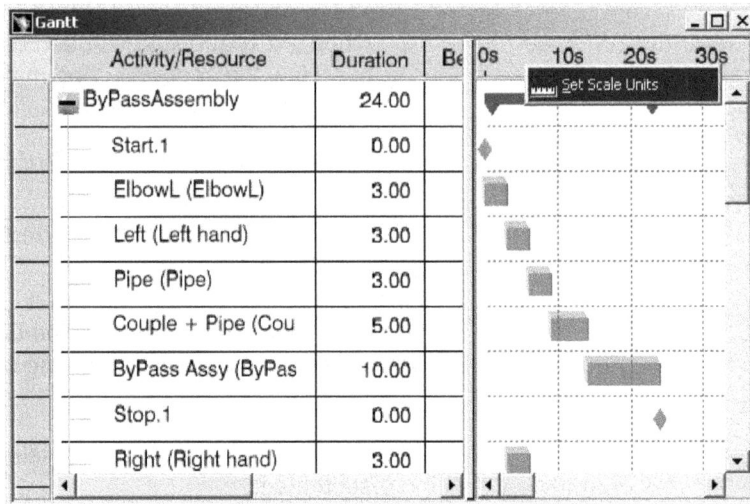

Activity/Resource	Duration
ByPassAssembly	24.00
Start.1	0.00
ElbowL (ElbowL)	3.00
Left (Left hand)	3.00
Pipe (Pipe)	3.00
Couple + Pipe (Cou	5.00
ByPass Assy (ByPas	10.00
Stop.1	0.00
Right (Right hand)	3.00

Figure 3–28

4. In the Set Scale Units dialog box, set the *Scale* to **2** as shown in Figure 3–29.

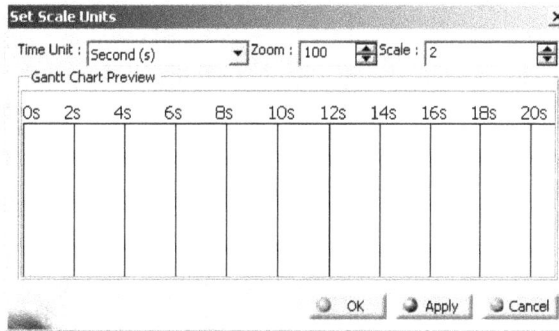

Figure 3–29

5. Click **OK**. The Gantt Chart opens as shown in Figure 3–30.

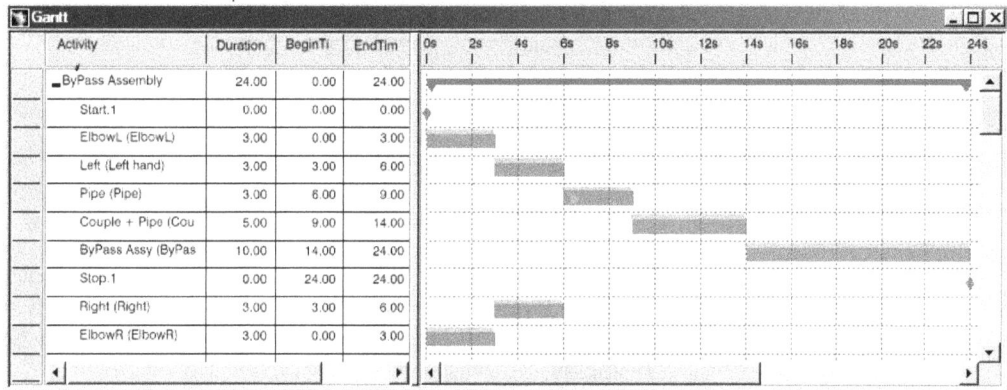

Figure 3–30

Task 4 - Change the durations and add delay to the sequence.

In this task, you will use the Gantt Chart to modify the duration and delay for fitting actions in the **ByPass Assembly** sequence.

Design Considerations

The fitting action duration and delay can be modified in two ways:

- Using the tabular data on the left side. This is useful when entering specific duration and delay values.

- Using the graphic interface on the right side. The entire track bar can be dragged to add a delay, or the ends of the track bar can be dragged to change the duration. This is useful when making quick changes to the sequence.

1. Change the duration of the **ByPass Assy** track by dragging the end of the track bar to the 20 second mark, as shown in Figure 3–31. This changes the duration of the track to approximately six seconds.

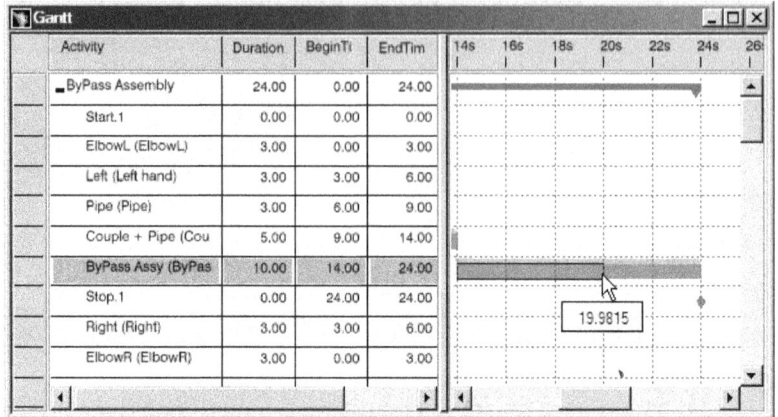

Figure 3–31

2. To enter a duration of exactly six seconds, double-click on the *Duration* cell for the **ByPass Assy** track and enter **6**.

3. Add a delay of approximately two seconds by dragging the entire **ByPass Assy** track bar to the position shown in Figure 3–32. If required, modify the *BeginTime* and *EndTime* values.

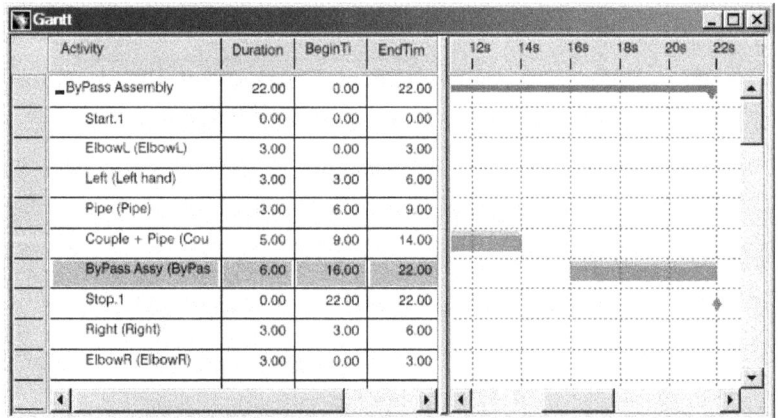

Figure 3–32

The Gantt Chart does not need to be saved. The modifications that are made to the chart are associatively updated in the assembly model. Therefore, once you have finished making changes to the chart, you can close the window. You must save the assembly to maintain the changes.

4. Click ☒ (Close) in the upper right corner to close the Gantt Chart window.

5. In the Piping.CATProduct window, double-click on the **ByPass Assembly** sequence to open the Sequence Editor dialog box.

    The modifications made to the Gantt Chart are also automatically made to the Sequence Editor. This associativity is maintained in the Gantt Chart when modifications are made using the Sequence Editor.

6. Close the Sequence Editor and save the assembly.

Task 5 - (Optional) Generate a video.

In this task, you will generate a video of the **ByPass Assembly** sequence. To review the generated video, you will require a video player application. Check with your instructor to confirm that an application is available before proceeding.

1. In the specification tree, preselect the **ByPass Assembly** sequence.

2. Select **Tools>Simulation>Generate Video**. The Video Generation dialog box opens as shown in Figure 3–33.

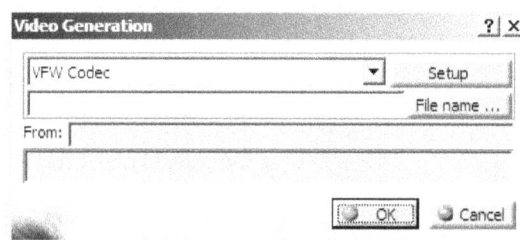

Figure 3–33

3. With the Video Generation dialog box still open, perform the following functions to simplify the display:

- Hide the Applications branch in the specification tree. This toggles off the display of tracks and shuttles.
- Select **View>Specifications** (or press <F3>) to toggle off the display of the specification tree.
- Select **View>Compass** to toggle off the display of the compass.
- It is also recommended that you resize the window to minimize the size of the video file created.
- Resize and reorient the model to best fit the window.

4. Select **VFW Codec** to define the type of video to be generated.

5. Click **Setup**. This dialog box enables you to specify the compressor (or codec) that is used to define the video output, and other quality settings. You will use the default settings to generate this video.

The default codec specified by Dassault generates very large files with lower image quality. It is recommended that you download and install a 3rd party codec to improve quality and reduce file size.

6. Close the Choose Compressor dialog box.

7. Click **File name** and save the AVI file in the *Piping* folder with the name **ByPass**.

8. Click **OK**. The system replays the sequence while saving the video information in the AVI file. Once the file creation is complete, the Video Generation dialog box closes.

9. Open Windows Explorer and browse to the *C:\DMU_Fitting_ Simulator_Exercise_Files\Piping* folder.

10. Double-click on **ByPass.avi** to review the video.

11. Once complete, close the video player and return to CATIA.

12. Restore the window size, specification tree, and compass.

13. Save the assembly and close the window.

Analysis Tools

In this chapter, you will learn how to use analysis tools to review the volume consumed by an object as it travels along a track. You will also learn how to conduct a clash analysis to check for interferences, and to perform experiments to analyze the results of an analysis at each time step of a sequence.

Learning Objectives in this Chapter

- Create a Swept Volume to store the volume that is consumed by an object as it travels along a track.
- Conduct a Space Analysis.
- Modify a Track.
- Perform an Experiment to analyze the results of an analysis at each time step of a sequence.

4.1 Create a Swept Volume

A swept volume enables you to store the volume that is consumed by an object as it travels along a track. This can be useful when you are trying to optimize the process of visualizing a variety of assembly scenarios. You can also perform clash analyses with the swept volume to see whether it interferes with the surrounding components.

The **Swept Volume** tool creates a CGR representation of all of the positions of a component as it moves along the length of a track. An example is shown in Figure 4–1.

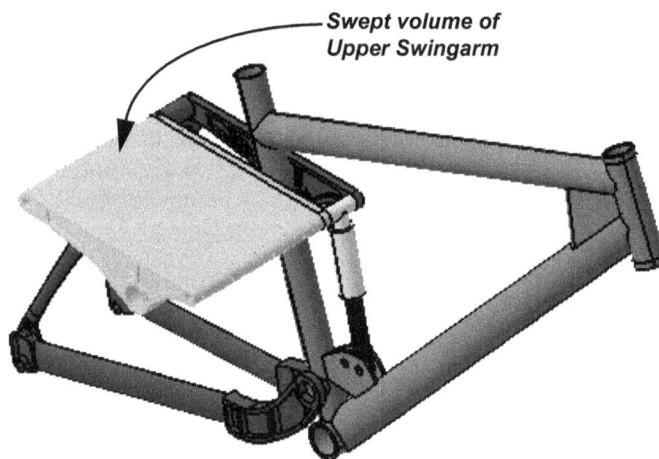

Swept volume of Upper Swingarm

Figure 4–1

General Steps

Use the following steps to create a swept volume:

1. Begin creation of a swept volume.
2. Specify parameters for the swept volume.
3. Complete the creation of the swept volume.

Step 1 - Begin creation of a swept volume.

To create a swept volume, click [icon] (Swept Volume) in the DMU Simulation toolbar. The Swept Volume dialog box opens as shown in Figure 4–2.

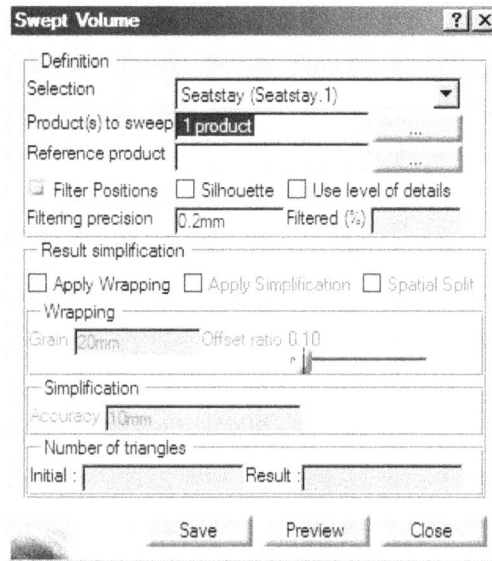

Figure 4–2

Step 2 - Specify parameters for the swept volume.

The **Selection** parameter must be defined to create a swept volume. This defines the track that is used to generate the volume. Select the track in the Selection drop-down list. The Product(s) to sweep automatically default to the object that has been added to the track.

Wrapping and simplification are possible if the DMU Optimizer license has been purchased.

Step 3 - Complete the creation of the swept volume.

Once the parameters have been specified, the swept volume can be generated. Click **Preview** to display the CGR representation in a separate window. Click **Save** to save the CGR file to the hard drive.

Once the CGR has been saved, it can be inserted into the mechanism by selecting **Insert>Existing Component**. This enables you to visualize the swept volume in the context of the rest of the assembly.

4.2 Space Analyses

You can perform three types of space analyses in the DMU Fitting workbench: Clash Tool, Clash Detection, and Distance & Band Analysis.

Clash Tool

This method of analyzing clash is identical to the use of the **Clash Analysis** tool in the Space Analysis workbench. The analysis is performed on the current positions of the components in the fitting simulation.

To use the **Clash** tool, click (Clash) in the DMU Check toolbar. The Clash dialog box opens as shown in Figure 4–3.

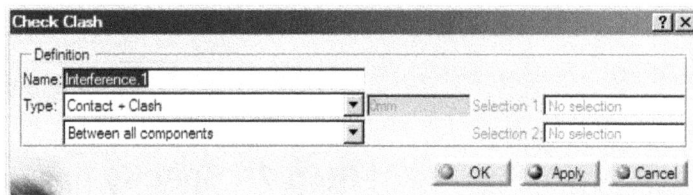

Figure 4–3

After selecting the parameters of the clash analysis, click **Apply** to calculate and review the results. Click **OK** to add the clash analysis to the specification tree if you have a DMU Space Analysis license.

Clash Detection

This type of clash analysis enables you to determine whether the interference exists between components throughout the movement defined by the fitting simulation. The clash detection tools are available in the **Automatic Clash Detection** flyout in the DMU Check toolbar, as shown in Figure 4–4. The three icons are described in the following table.

Figure 4–4

Option	Description
![icon] (Clash Detection (Off))	No clash analysis is performed. This is the default option.
![icon] (Clash Detection (On))	The next time the assembly is simulated using a sequence or replay, any detected areas of clash are highlighted in red.
![icon] (Clash Detection (Stop))	The next time the assembly is simulated using a sequence or replay, the simulation stops when a clash is detected.

Distance & Band Analysis

This analysis method is identical to the use of the **Distance & Band Analysis** tool in the Space Analysis workbench. This tool enables you to measure the minimum X-, Y-, or Z-distance between components in a product (distance analysis). Additionally, you can compute and visualize areas of a product that correspond to the minimum and maximum distance as defined by the user (band analysis).

To access the **Distance & Band Analysis** tool, click

![icon] (Distance and Band Analysis) in the DMU Check toolbar. The Edit Distance and Band Analysis dialog box opens as shown in Figure 4–5. The analysis is performed on the current positions of the components in the fitting simulation.

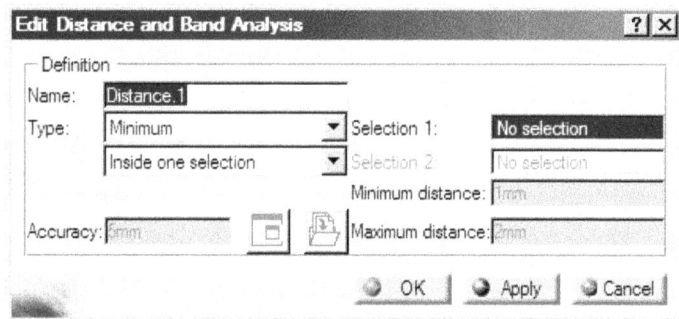

Figure 4–5

4.3 Modify a Track

The **Path Finder** tool is used to modify an existing track to eliminate clash conditions between the object and the surrounding components in the assembly.

The system calculates the new path using an iterative process. The object is moved down the track and the system performs a clash analysis between the object and the surrounding models. If clash is detected, the system uses the penetration depth to move the component and eliminate the clash. The new object position is recorded as a point in the new path. This process is repeated until the object reaches the end of the track. All of the points are then joined with curves to develop the new track.

For example, a track has been defined for the **Screw** object shown in Figure 4–6. This track causes the **Screw** to come into a clash situation with the **Handle**.

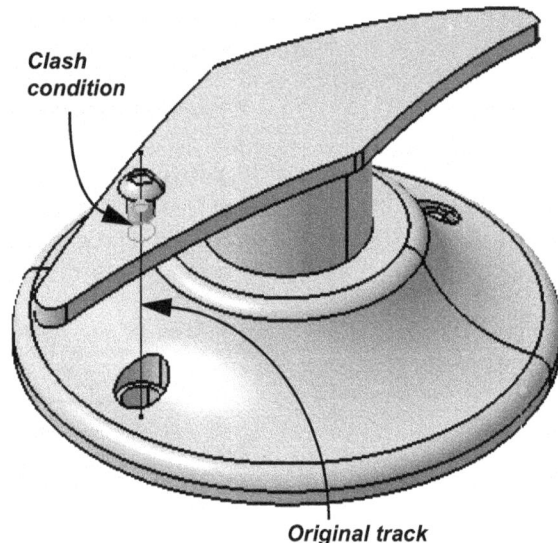

Clash condition

Original track

Figure 4–6

The **Path Finder** tool can be used to develop a path that avoids this clash condition. An example of a track that was modified using the **Path Finder** tool is shown in Figure 4–7.

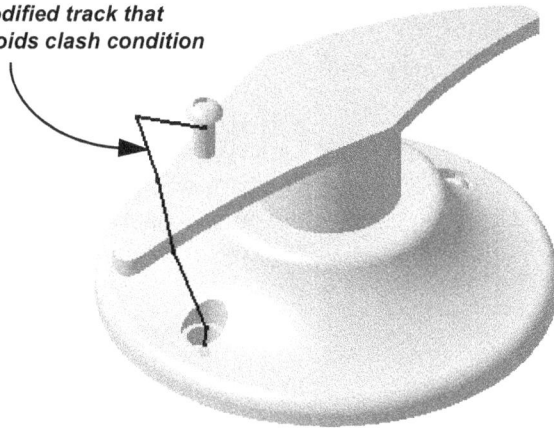

Modified track that avoids clash condition

Figure 4–7

General Steps

Use the following general steps to modify a track using the **Path Finder** tool:

1. Develop a track.
2. Start the **Path Finder** tool.
3. Modify the path finder boundary, if required.
4. Specify the parameters of the **Path Finder** operation.
5. Create the new track.
6. (Optional) Smooth the new track.

Step 1 - Develop a track.

The **Path Finder** tool works from an existing track to determine the intended path of the object. Therefore, a track must already be present before you start the **Path Finder** operation. As a minimum, the track shows the system the start and end position of the object. However, the track also influences the direction of the path finder and should therefore approximate the completed track as closely as possible.

For the **Path Finder** tool to be used on a track, the track must encounter a clash condition at one location along its length. Ideally, the track should not start or end in a clash condition. If the track starts with a clash condition, it can be ignored using the **Ignore collisions** option in the Path Finder dialog box.

Step 2 - Start the Path Finder tool.

To begin the **Path Finder** operation, click [icon] (Path Finder) in the DMU Check toolbar. The Select dialog box opens, displaying all of the tracks that have been added to the simulation, as shown in Figure 4–8. Select the track to be modified and click **OK**.

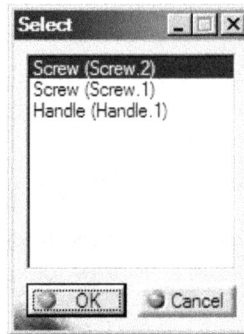

Select

Screw (Screw.2)
Screw (Screw.1)
Handle (Handle.1)

OK   Cancel

Figure 4–8

Once this is done, the boundary displays on the model and the Path Finder dialog box opens as shown in Figure 4–9.

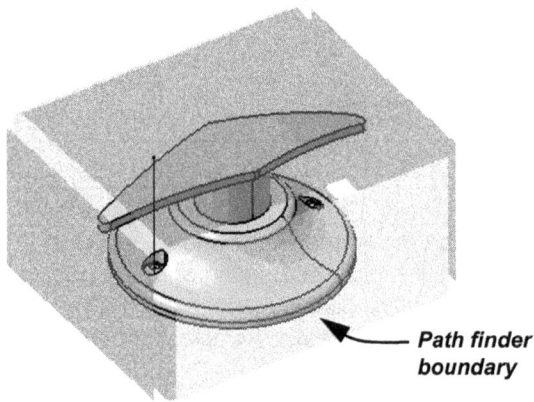

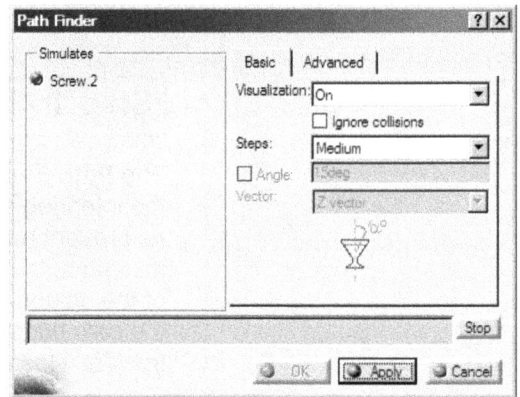

— Path finder
boundary

Path Finder

Simulates
Screw.2

Basic | Advanced

Visualization: On

☐ Ignore collisions

Steps: Medium

☐ Angle: 1.5deg

Vector: Z vector

Stop

OK   Apply   Cancel

Figure 4–9

Step 3 - Modify the path finder boundary, if required.

The boundary provides a visual display of the volume in which the path finder can move the object to avoid the clash condition in the path. The boundary can be modified by selecting a boundary surface and dragging it to a new location.

Using the views in the Quick View toolbar is useful for displaying 2D orientations of the model and positioning the boundary more accurately, as shown in Figure 4–10.

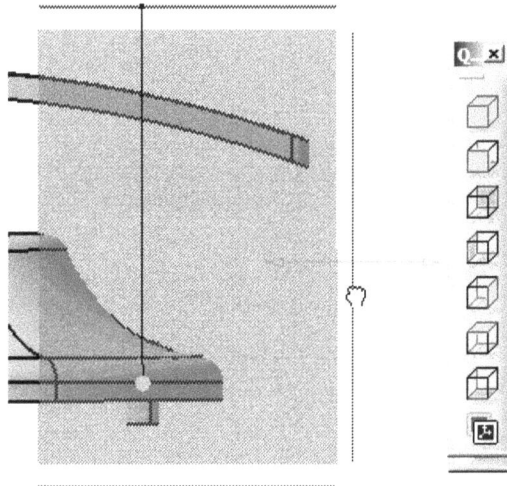

Figure 4–10

Step 4 - Specify the parameters of the Path Finder operation.

The Path Finder dialog box contains two tabs. The options in the *Basic* tab and the options in the *Advanced* tab are described as follows:

- Basic Tab

Option	Description
Visualization	Controls the display of the object during the **Path Finder** operation. There are three options: • **On:** The object displays during the operation and the process can be stopped by clicking **Stop**. • **Off:** The object is not displayed during the operation and the process cannot be stopped. • **Strombo (1/20):** The model is updated at every 20th position calculated by the path finder.
Ignore Collisions	Enables the system to ignore a clash condition occurring at the start of the track that is being modified.
Steps	Controls the size of the step down the track taken by the path finder. A smaller step is typically able to produce a track that closely matches the original track. However, a smaller step also increases the resources required to produce the track and therefore takes longer to calculate. There are four options in the Steps drop-down list: • Small • Medium • Large • **Advanced:** The step size is manually defined using options in the *Advanced* tab.
Validation options	If the object for the track being modified is a shuttle that uses validation options to control its orientation, the **Angle** option is selected and the validation values are reported at the bottom of the *Basic* tab. These values always remain grayed out because they are controlled using the Shuttle dialog box.

- Advanced Tab

Option	Description
Environment	
Smallest detail	When the path finder runs, it builds an environment of possible locations to which the object can move. This option controls the smallest entity that the system considers to be part of the environment. For example, if this value is larger than the diameter of a hole in the model, the hole is not included in the environment and the object is not capable of moving into the space created by the hole. As the value is decreased, the accuracy of the operation and the required computational resources increases.
Repulse effect	Controls the impact of a clash condition on the **Path Finder** operation. A value of **High** moves the object further away when a clash condition is detected, resulting in a smooth path that is calculated faster. A value of **Low** results in a longer calculation that closely matches the original path.
Bounding box	There are three options in the Bounding box drop-down list: • **Environment:** The bounding box is defined to enclose the entire model. • **Path:** The bounding box is defined to enclose the path being operated on. • **Custom:** The bounding box has been modified by dragging the sides of the box.
Motion	These options control the step size when Advanced is selected in the Steps drop-down list in the *Basic* tab.
Translation step	The size of the step when translating the object.
Rotation gain	This option controls the angular step when rotating the object. The value entered is multiplied by the Translation step value to determine the angular step size.
Apply to part of the track	Enables you to select a portion of a track that is modified by the path finder. If this option is selected, you must specify a start and end point on the track before running the Path Finder operation.

Step 5 - Create the new track.

To run the **Path Finder** operation, click **Apply**. The system begins to calculate the new path. The Path Finder dialog box displays the progress of the operation, as shown in Figure 4–11.

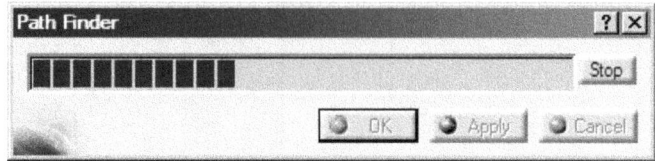

Figure 4–11

Once the process has completed, click **OK**. The system hides the old path and the newly created path displays on the model. The **Path Finder** operation is also reported in the specification tree, as shown in Figure 4–12.

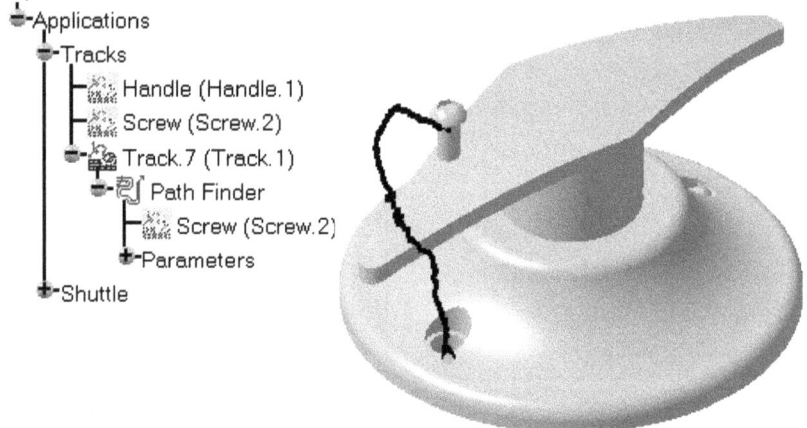

Figure 4–12

Step 6 - (Optional) Smooth the new track.

The **Smooth** tool is used to smooth any track to provide a more natural assembly path. This is most useful when you are working with the **Path Finder** tool because the resulting track is very disjointed and rough as it was developed using lines that connect each of the calculated points.

How To: Smooth a Track

1. In the DMU Check toolbar, click (Smooth).
2. Select the new track generated by the path finder in the Select dialog box. The Smooth dialog box opens as shown in Figure 4–13.

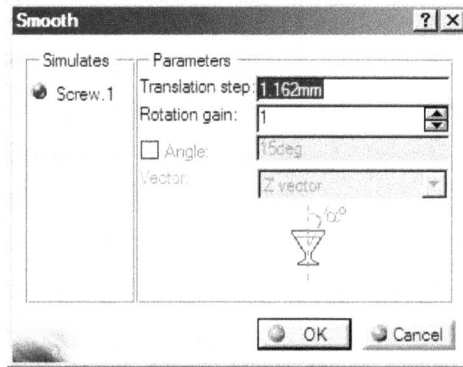

Figure 4–13

3. If required, enter values for the *Translation step* and *Rotation gain*. The smaller the value, the longer the **Smooth** operation takes and the closer the resulting track matches the original path.
4. Click **OK** to perform the **Smooth** operation. Once completed, the newly smoothed track displays on the model. The specification tree indicates that a **Smoothing** operation has been performed, as shown in Figure 4–14.

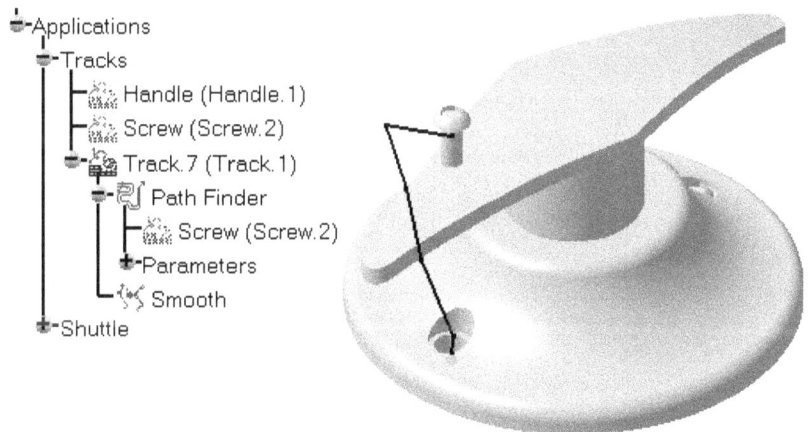

Figure 4–14

Depending on the track, *Translation step*, and *Rotational gain* values entered, the system might smooth the path so that a clash condition could reoccur. Therefore, you should always play the new track in a sequence with clash detection enabled. If a clash does occur, adjust the parameters of the **Path Finder** or **Smooth** operation to eliminate the clash.

To automatically perform a **Smooth** operation when running the path finder, enable the **Automatic Smooth after Path Finder execution** option (**Tools>Options>Digital Mockup>DMU Fitting>***DMU Fitting* tab), as shown in Figure 4–15.

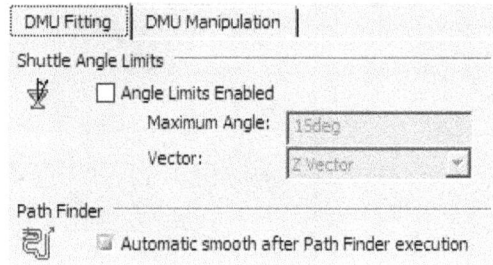

Figure 4–15

4.4 Perform an Experiment

An experiment enables you to analyze the results of an analysis at each time step of a sequence. The system reports the value of these sensors (for example: distances, measures, or interference data) at each step of a sequence. The data can then be displayed in tabular or graphical formats.

For example, a measurement is created for the minimum distance between the **Turbine Blade** and **Diffuser Housing** components shown in Figure 4–16. Using an experiment, the value of this measurement is reported during a sequence that moves the **Diffuser Housing** toward the blade. When the experiment is run, the measurement is reported in an Excel spreadsheet and can also be graphed in DMU Fitting.

~153.852mm

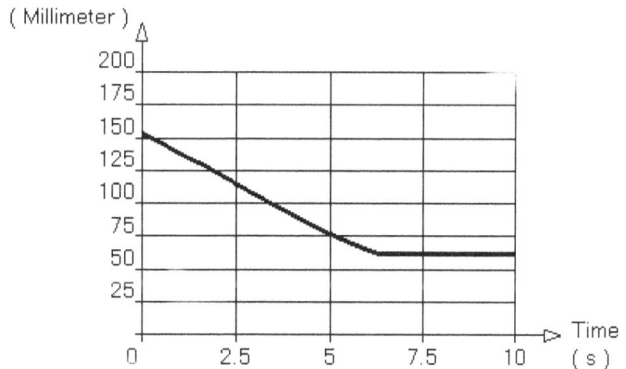

	A	B
1	Time.1 (s)	`DISTANCE.1\Minimal Distance` (mm)
2	0	153.8519897
3	0.1	152.2854767
4	0.2	150.726532
5	0.3	149.1753693
6	0.4	147.6322479
7	0.5	146.09729
8	0.6	144.5707092
9	0.7	143.0518188
10	0.8	141.5402985
11	0.9	140.0380402
12	1	138.5453186

Figure 4–16

General Steps	Use the following general steps to perform an experiment:

1. Define the sensors to be measured.
2. Start the **Edit & Perform Experiment** tool.
3. Select the sensors to be observed.
4. Review the results of the experiment.

Step 1 - Define the sensors to be measured.

Before performing an experiment, your assembly model should already have the required shuttles, fitting actions, and sequences defined.

You must also define any sensors that you want to analyze using the experiment. A sensor is any type of measurement that can be created using the following analysis tools:

- Measurements using (Measure Between) or (Measure Item). The **Keep Measure** option in the Measure dialog box must be selected to use this type of sensor in an experiment.

- Clash analysis using the **Clash** tool. The system analyzes the penetration or clearance value reported by the analysis. The **Compute penetration depth or minimum distance** option for During Initial Computation (**Tools>Options> Digital Mockup>DMU Space Analysis** and then select the *DMU Clash* tab) must be enabled.

- Distance & Band Analysis

Once these sensors have been created, you must modify the sequence to analyze them. This is done by double-clicking on the sequence in the specification tree to open the Edit Sequence dialog box. Select the *Analysis* tab and move the required sensors into the field, as shown in Figure 4–17.

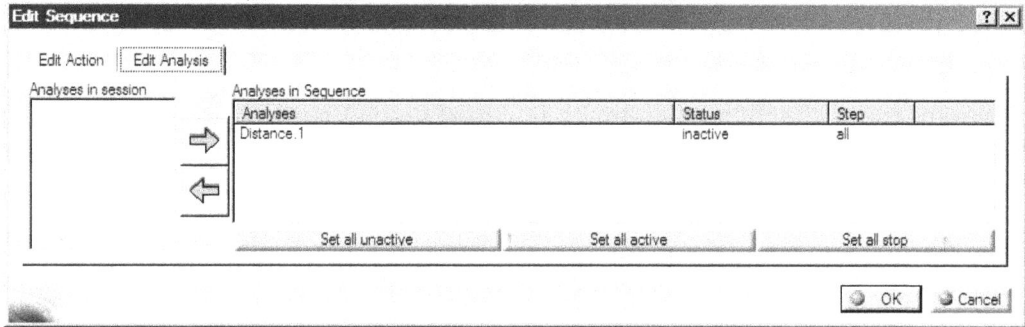

Figure 4–17

Step 2 - Start the Edit & Perform Experiment tool.

To start the definition of an experiment, select the sequence that is going to be analyzed and click ▦ (Edit & Perform Experiment). The dialog box opens as shown in Figure 4–18. It displays all of the sensors that have been added to the selected sequence.

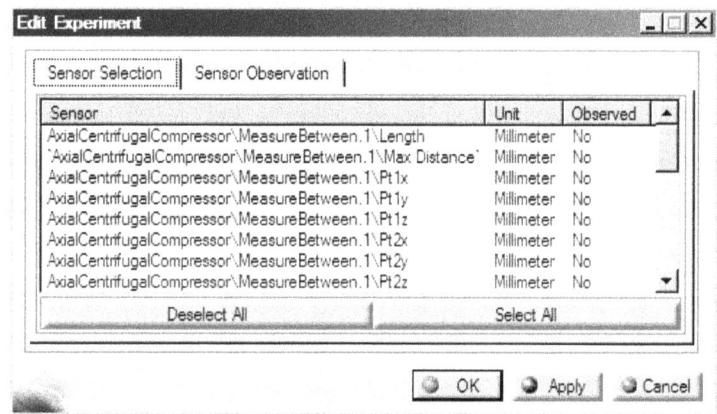

Figure 4–18

Step 3 - Select the sensors to be observed.

By default, all of the sensors are disabled. To enable specific sensors, select them from the list to toggle the **Observed** value to **Yes**. Click **Select All** to enable all of the sensors, as shown in Figure 4-19.

Select the sensor to toggle the Observed status

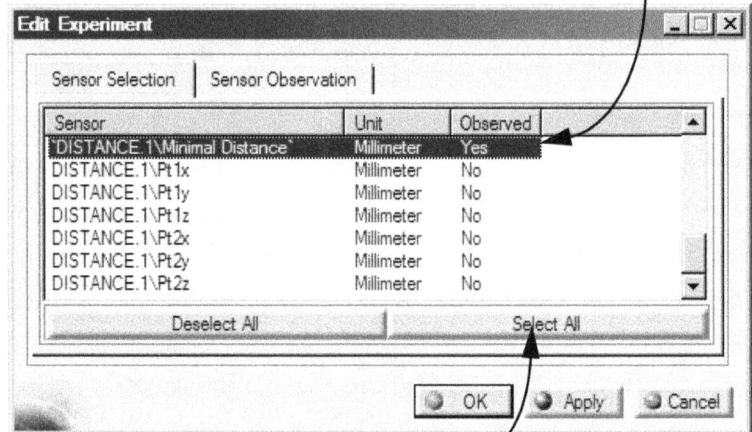

Select this button to activate all sensors

Figure 4-19

To disable a sensor, select it from the list to toggle the *Observed* value to **No**. Click **Deselect All** to disable all of the sensors.

Step 4 - Review the results of the experiment.

You can review the results of an experiment in two ways:

- Instantaneous Results

- Stored Results

Instantaneous Results

This method enables you to display the change in the sensors as the system replays the sequence. These results are not stored anywhere for future access. The values are only available while the Edit Experiment dialog box is open.

How To: Review the Instantaneous Results of an Experiment

1. Select the *Sensor Observation* tab. It displays all of the active sensors and their current values, as shown in Figure 4–20.

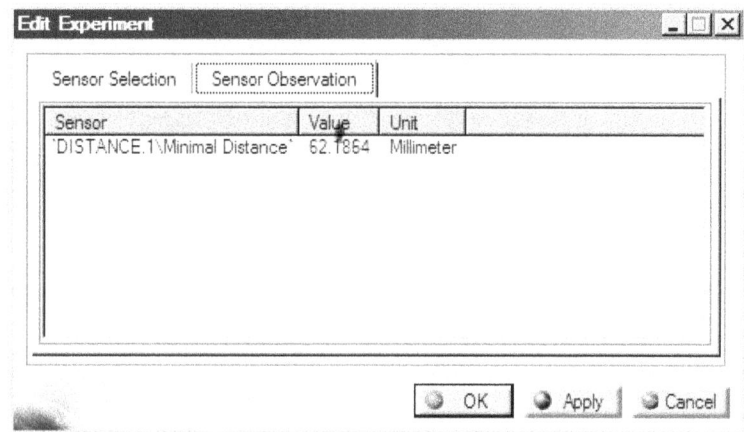

Figure 4–20

2. Use the Player toolbar to play the sequence. As the sequence progresses, the values of the sensors update in the Edit Experiment dialog box.

Stored Results

This method enables you to store the sensor data so that all of the values can be reviewed graphically at a later time.

How To: Store the Results of an Experiment

1. Click **Apply**. The Save As dialog box opens, enabling you to save the results in an Excel spreadsheet (*.XLS) or a text file (*.TXT).
2. Enter a descriptive name for the results file and save it to your system. The system generates the experiment results by replaying the sequence and capturing the results data at each step.

3. Once the results have been generated, the Browse Experiment dialog box opens as shown in Figure 4–21.

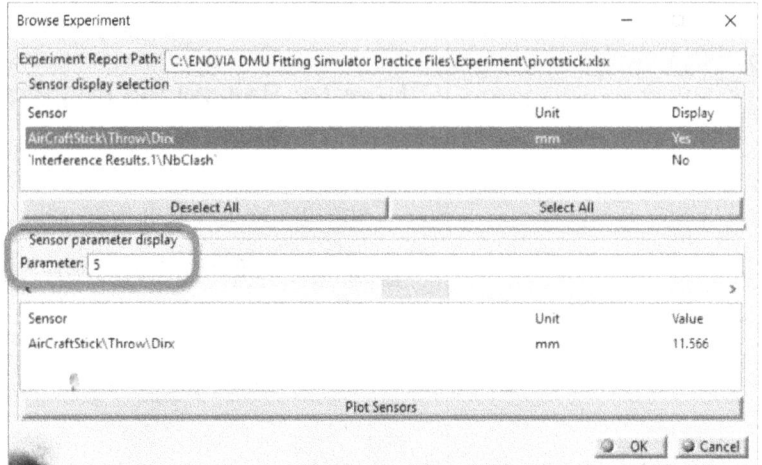

Figure 4–21

The results for the selected sensors can be displayed at a specific time step by entering the value in the *Parameter* field. Otherwise, the slider bar under the *Parameter* field can be dragged to a required time step.

To plot the selected sensors over the entire time range, click **Plot Sensors**. The Sensor Display dialog box opens as shown in Figure 4–22.

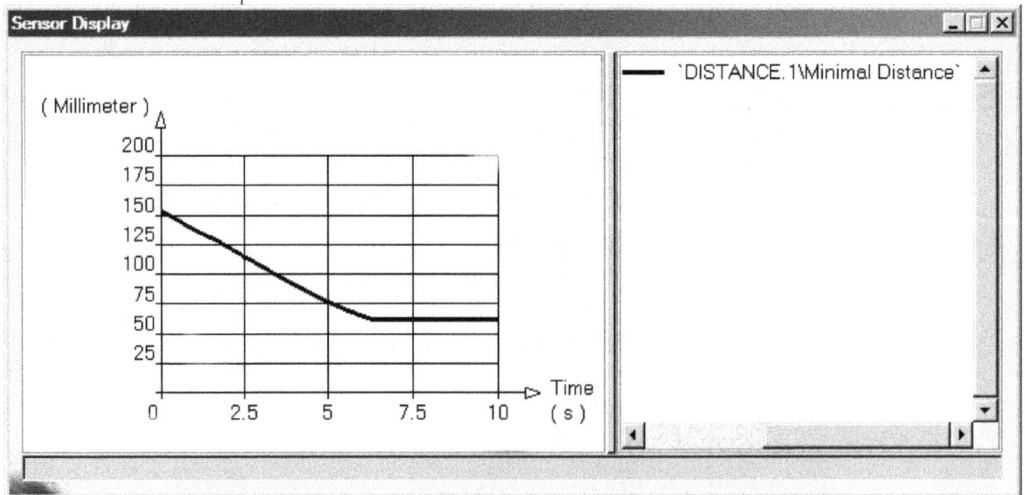

Figure 4–22

Once you have finished reviewing the experiment, close the dialog boxes. The system adds the experiment to the specification tree, as shown in Figure 4–23. The experiment can be accessed by double-clicking on the experiment in the tree.

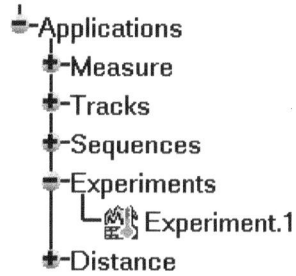

Figure 4–23

Practice 4a | Path Finder

Practice Objectives

- Use the Path Finder tool to modify a track.
- Use the Smooth tool to smooth a rough track.

In this task, you will use the **Path Finder** to modify an existing track to avoid a clash condition. The linear disassembly of two **Screws** creates a clash condition with the **Handle** component, as shown in Figure 4–24.

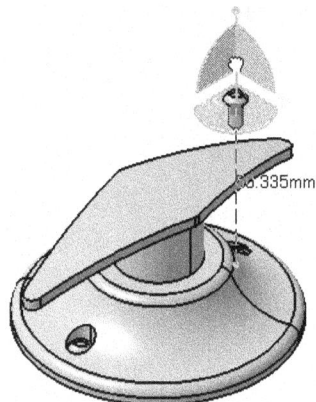

Figure 4–24

The **Path Finder** approximates two new paths that avoid the **Handle** component. The first **Path Finder** operation uses the default options, while the second works with a shuttle that has validation settings. The resulting paths display as shown in Figure 4–25.

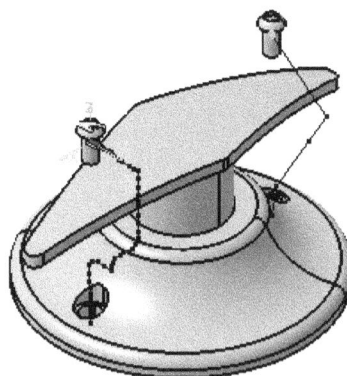

Figure 4–25

Task 1 - Open an assembly model.

1. Open **DoorHandle.CATProduct** from the *PathFinder* directory. The model displays as shown in Figure 4–26.

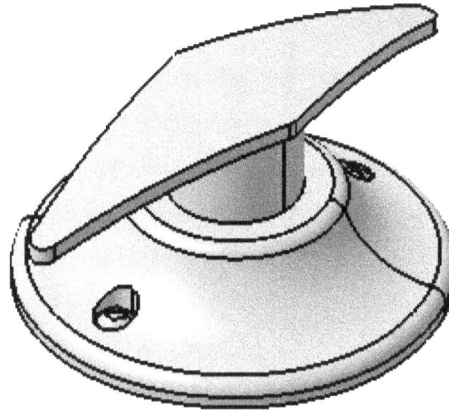

Figure 4–26

2. Investigate the assembly. The model consists of four components. The **Handle** is assembled into the **Bezel** component and is then mounted using two **Screws**. You are creating a simulation that displays the disassembly of these **Screws**.

Task 2 - Create a track.

In this task, you will create a track that moves one of the **Screw** components upwards so that it clashes with the **Handle** component. You will then use the **Path Finder** tool to automatically create a track that does not intersect the **Handle**. This operation is for demonstration purposes only, because the **Handle** component would be rotated out of the way to avoid the clash.

1. Create a track named **Screw No Validation** and select **Screw.1** as the object.

2. Drag the object upward by approximately **50mm** to the position shown in Figure 4–27.

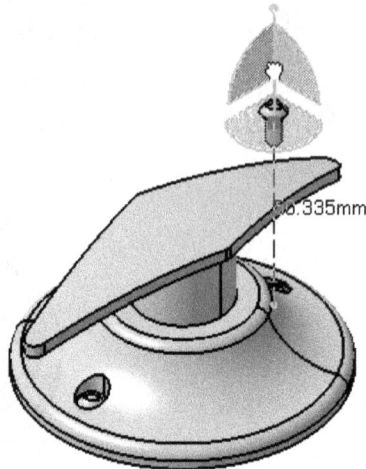

Figure 4–27

3. Click ⊞ (Record Insert) to insert a shot.

4. Set the *mode* to **Time** and enter **10s**.

5. Complete the track creation.

Task 3 - Use the path finder to avoid the clash condition.

---

1. In the DMU Check toolbar, click ⬚ (Path Finder). The Select dialog box opens, displaying the tracks that have been created in the model. Only one track currently exists, as shown in Figure 4–28.

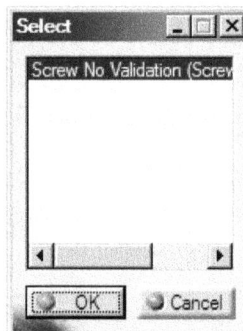

Figure 4–28

2. Select the **Screw No Validation** track and click **OK**. The Path
   Finder dialog box opens. The system also displays the
   bounding box for the **Path Finder** operation on the model, as
   shown in Figure 4–29.

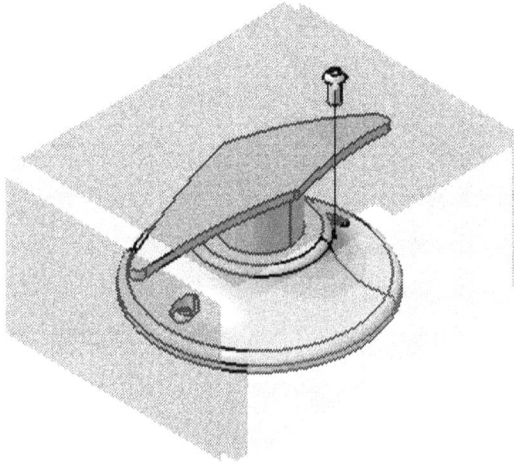

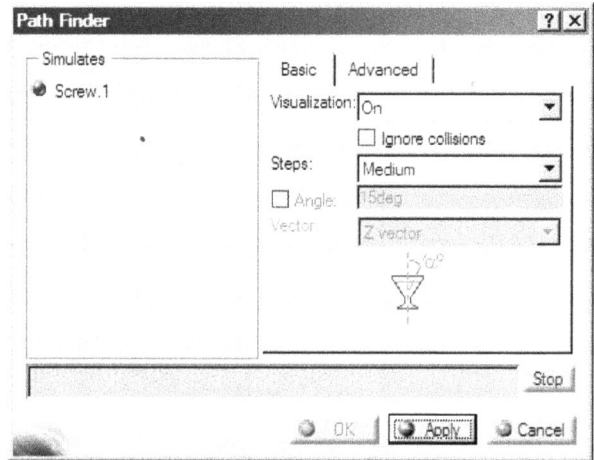

Figure 4–29

3. Ensure that the following parameters are set:

   - *Visualization:* **On**
   - *Ignore collisions:* **Clear this option**
   - *Steps:* **Medium**

Design Considerations

By default, the **Bounding box** option is set to **Environment** so
that it encompasses the entire model. This enables the **Path
Finder** to position the component anywhere around the model.
You can restrict the movement of the object by modifying the
bounding box. For example, in the case of the screw, you can
modify the box so that the component can only move in the Y-
and Z-directions.

To change the bounding box, select on a face and drag it to a
new position.

1. Select the *Advanced* tab.

2. In the Bounding box drop-down list, select **Path**. The boundary is now set to contain the **Screw No Validation** path, as shown in Figure 4–30.

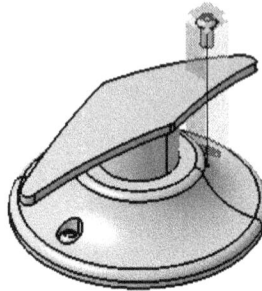

Figure 4–30

3. Drag the front face of the bounding box so that it displays as shown in Figure 4–31.

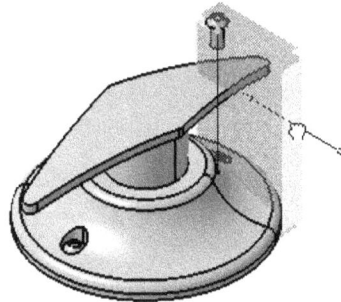

Figure 4–31

4. Click **Apply** to initiate the **Path Finder** operation. The system begins to adjust the position and orientation of the component as it moves along the **Screw No Validation** path. Once complete, the new path displays as a preview on the model, as shown in Figure 4–32.

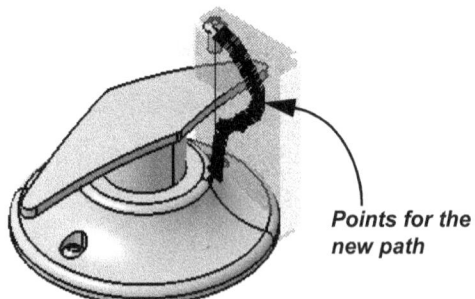

Points for the new path

Figure 4–32

5. Click **OK** to create the new path. The system hides the original **Screw No Validation** path and positions it under the new path in the specification tree, as shown in Figure 4–33.

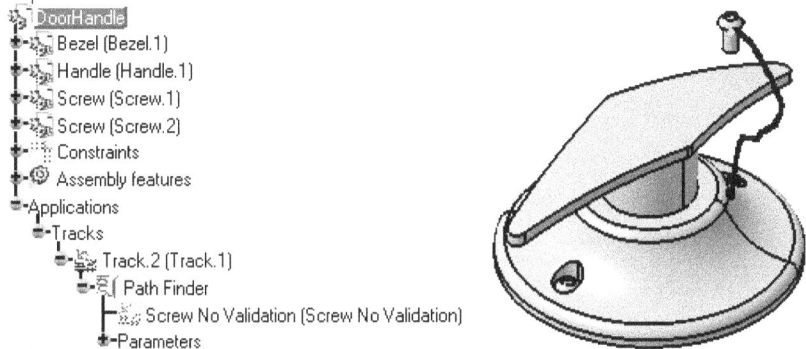

Figure 4–33

6. Rename **Track.2** as **Screw NV Path**.

Task 4 - Smooth the track.

---

1. In the DMU Check toolbar, click (Smooth). The Select dialog box opens.

2. Select **Screw NV Path** and click **OK**. The Smooth dialog box opens as shown in Figure 4–34.

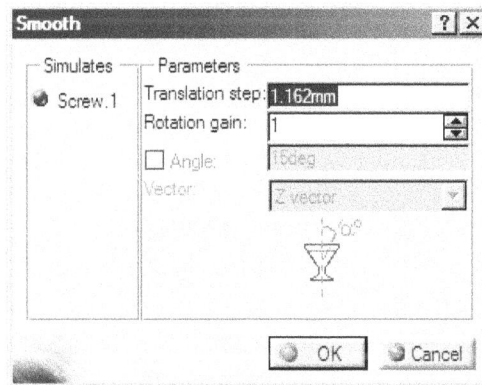

Figure 4–34

3. Accept the default settings and click **OK**. The resulting smoothed curve displays as shown in Figure 4–35.

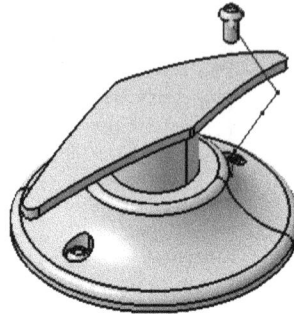

Figure 4–35

Design Considerations

The **Smooth** tool does not take the clash conditions avoided in the **Path Finder** operation into consideration. Therefore, it might be possible that a clash condition has been recreated during the **Smooth** operation. It is recommended that you perform a clash detection analysis before accepting the **Smooth** operation. If clash is detected, the parameters of the **Smooth** operation can be modified, or the smoothing can be removed by deleting the Smooth branch from beneath the track in the specification tree.

4. Create a sequence and add the **Screw NV Path** track.

5. In the DMU Simulation toolbar, expand the Automatic Clash Detection flyout and click (Clash Detection **Stop**). This stops the sequence when a clash is detected.

6. Play the sequence. The sequence should complete successfully, indicating that the **Smooth** tool did not cause a clash condition. The path finder created a new track and the duration settings were not maintained from the **Screw No Validation** track.

7. Click **Cancel** to exit without creating the sequence.

Task 5 - Create a shuttle.

In this task, you will repeat the **Path Finder** operation for the other **Screw**. This time, you will create a shuttle to invoke the **Validation** functionality, so that the system is limited by the amount of rotation it can apply during the **Path Finder** operation. The **Validation** functionality is located in the Shuttle dialog box.

1. Create a shuttle named **Screw** and add **Screw.2**.

2. Enable the **Angle** option and enter the following parameters:

   - *Angle:* **0deg**
   - *Vector:* **Z vector**

   The Shuttle dialog box opens as shown in Figure 4–36.

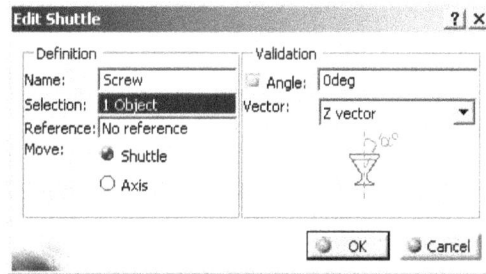

Figure 4–36

3. Click **OK** to complete the creation of the shuttle.

Task 6 - Create a track.

---

1. Create a track named **Screw Validation** and add the Screw shuttle as the object.

2. Drag the shuttle to a similar position to that used in the **Screw No Validation** track (approximately 50mm upwards over 10 seconds) and insert a shot.

3. Complete the creation of the track.

Task 7 - Perform a Path Finder and Smooth operation.

---

1. Click (Path Finder) and select the **Screw Validation** track.

2. Make the following selections in the Path Finder dialog box:

   - *Visualization:* **On**
   - *Steps:* **Large**

   Although the **Validation** options are grayed out in the Path Finder dialog box, the settings reflect those made previously in the Shuttle dialog box.

3. Modify the bounding box, as shown in Figure 4–37.

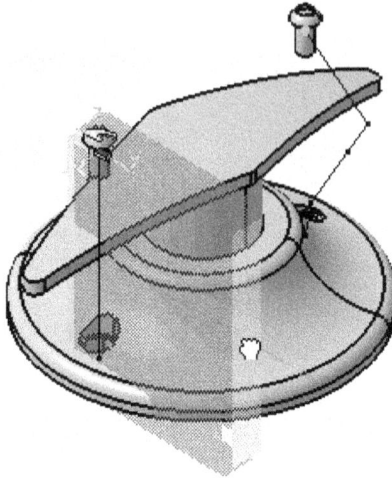

Figure 4–37

4. Click **Apply** to perform the **Path Finder** operation. The system obeys the defined validation settings and the **Screw** is not rotated at all throughout the operation.

5. Once the operation is complete, click **OK**. The resulting path displays as shown in Figure 4–38.

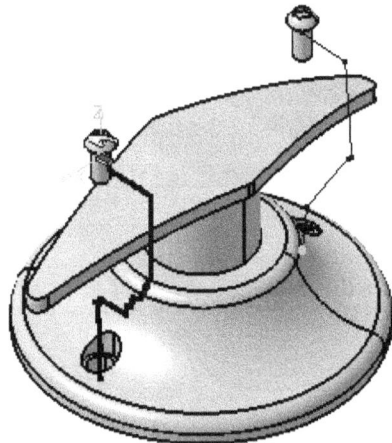

Figure 4–38

6. Rename the new track as **Screw Valid Path**.

7. Smooth **Screw Valid Path** using the default Translation step. The modified track displays as shown in Figure 4–39. Note the effect of the **Validation** options on the resulting track.

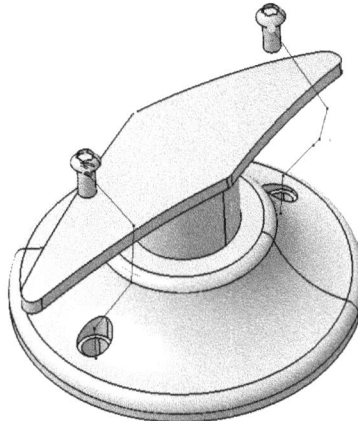

Figure 4–39

Task 8 - Create a new sequence.

1. Create a new sequence and add both tracks to the same step.

2. Set the duration for both actions to **10s**.

3. Play the sequence.

4. Click **OK**.

5. Save the model and close the window.

Practice 4b

Experiment

Practice Objective

- Define sensors and add them to a sequence.
- Perform an experiment.
- Create a swept volume.

In this practice, you will use the Experiment functionality in the DMU Fitting workbench. You will determine several critical pieces of engineering information about the **Aircraft Flight Stick** assembly shown in Figure 4–40.

Figure 4–40

As the **Flight Stick** is moved, the bottom comes into contact with four switches as shown in Figure 4–41. These switches send signals to a processor.

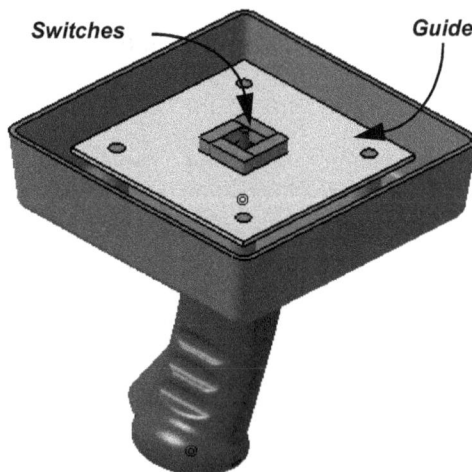

Figure 4–41

The designer of this **Flight Stick** has requested an analysis to determine the following parameters:

- The throw distance at the top of the stick at the contact position.

- Detect the clash between the **Flight Stick** and the **Base** and **Guide** components.

Task 1 - Open an assembly model.

1. Open **AirCraftStick.CATProduct** from the *Experiment* directory. The model displays as shown in Figure 4–42.

Figure 4–42

2. Ensure that you are in the DMU Fitting workbench ( ). To access this workbench, select **Start>Digital Mockup>DMU Fitting**.

3. Investigate the assembly. The model consists of a **Stick** component that sits in a **Base** and is connected with a spherical interface. The base of the **Stick** has a connector that comes in contact with four switches that interpret the directional inputs from the user.

4. In the specification tree, expand the Applications branch. The model contains a track and a sequence, as shown in Figure 4–43.

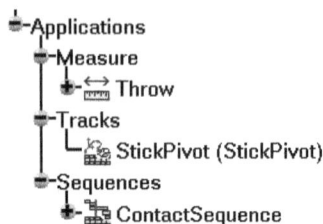

Figure 4–43

A measurement named **Throw** has been defined that calculates the throw distance of the **Stick**. This is the amount of play that a user encounters before any directional input is recorded by a switch.

Task 2 - Create a sensor.

In this task, you will create an additional sensor. This sensor will track the clash between the **Stick** and the four sensor components.

1. In the DMU Check toolbar, click (Clash). The Clash dialog box opens as shown in Figure 4–44.

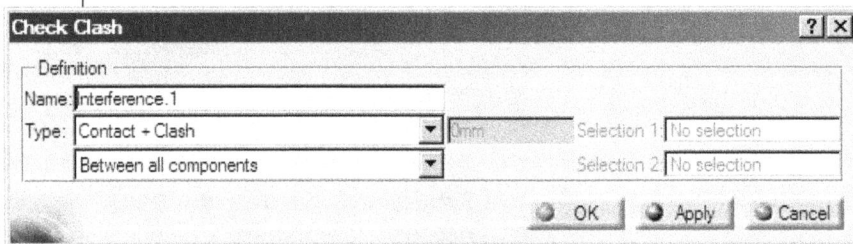

Figure 4–44

2. Make the following selections:

    *   *Name:* **Clash**
    *   *Type:* **Contact + Clash**, **Between two selections**
    *   *Selection 1:* (select this part) **Stick.1**
    *   *Selection 2:* (select these parts) **Switch.1-Switch.4**, select all four instances

The Check Clash dialog box opens as shown in Figure 4–45.

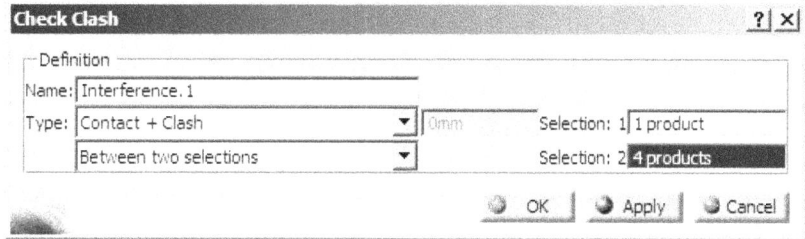

Check Clash   ? X

┌─ Definition ──
Name: | Interference. 1 |

Type: | Contact + Clash ▼ | 0mm   Selection: 1 | 1 product
      | Between two selections ▼ | Selection: 2 | 4 products |

                              ● OK   ● Apply   ● Cancel

Figure 4–45

3. Click **Apply** to apply the clash analysis and **OK** to close the
   Check Clash dialog box. The clash analysis is added to the
   Applications branch in the specification tree, as shown in
   Figure 4–46.

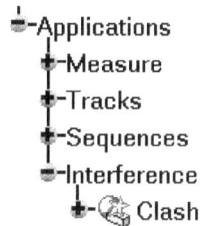

    ●-Applications
        ●-Measure
        ●-Tracks
        ●-Sequences
        ●-Interference
            ●-⬚ Clash

Figure 4–46

Task 3 - Modify the sequence.

In this task, you will modify the sequence to add the clash and
throw sensors.

1. In the specification tree, expand the Sequences branch and
   double-click on **ContactSequence**. The Edit Sequence
   dialog box opens.

2. Select the *Edit Analysis* tab, as shown in Figure 4–47.

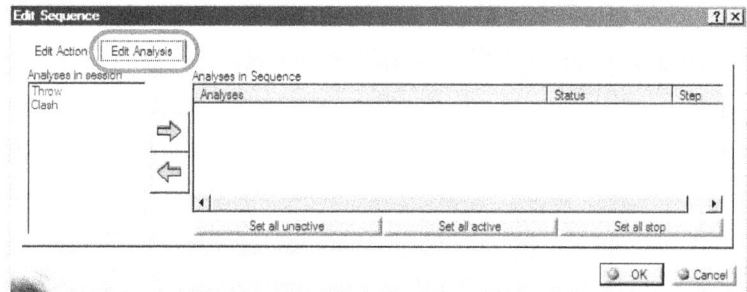

Edit Sequence   ? X

Edit Action | Edit Analysis |

Analyses in session   Analyses in Sequence
Throw   Analyses   Status   Step
Clash
                      ⇨

                      ⇦

                    ◄ │   │ ►
              Set all unactive   Set all active   Set all stop

                                            ● OK   ● Cancel

Figure 4–47

3. Use <Ctrl> to select **Throw** and **Clash** and click ⬜ to add the sensors to the *Analyses in Sequence* field. These sensors are now available when an experiment is run.

4. In the Player toolbar, click ⬜ (Parameters) and ensure that the *Sampling Step* is **1s**.

5. Click **OK**.

Task 4 - Create an experiment.

---

1. In the specification tree, select **ContactSequence**.

2. In the DMU Simulation toolbar, click ⬜ (Edit & Perform Experiment). The Edit Experiment dialog box opens as shown in Figure 4–48. It displays all of the parameters that are associated with the analyses that have been added to the selected sequence. These parameters are called sensors.

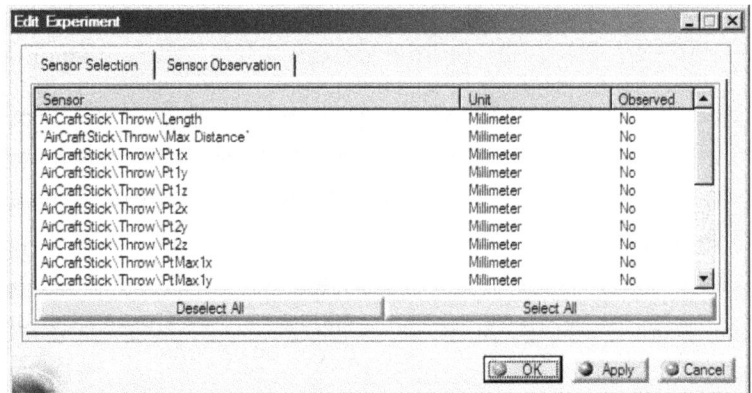

Figure 4–48

Design Considerations

Only add the required sensors to an experiment (recommended). The run time for an experiment increases with the number of sensors added.

3. Select the following sensors to be observed in the experiment, as shown in Figure 4–49:

   - **AirCraftStick\Throw\Dirx**
   - **Interference Results.1\NbClash**

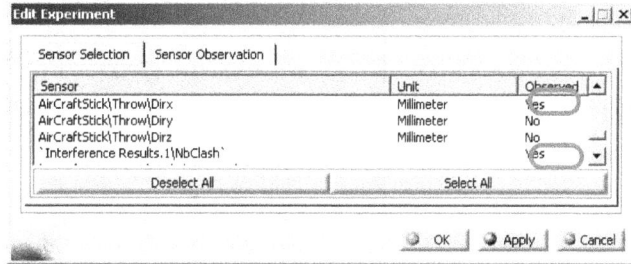

Figure 4–49

4. Click **Apply** and save the file as **PivotStick.xls** in the default directory.

Design Considerations

The system prompts you to save the Excel spreadsheet that contains the experiment data. Once the file has been created, the system begins to perform the experiment. The system starts to play the sequence while monitoring all of the observed sensors.

Task 5 - Analyze the experiment.

Once the experiment is complete, the Browse Experiment dialog box opens as shown in Figure 4–50. The top field displays the sensors that were added to the experiment.

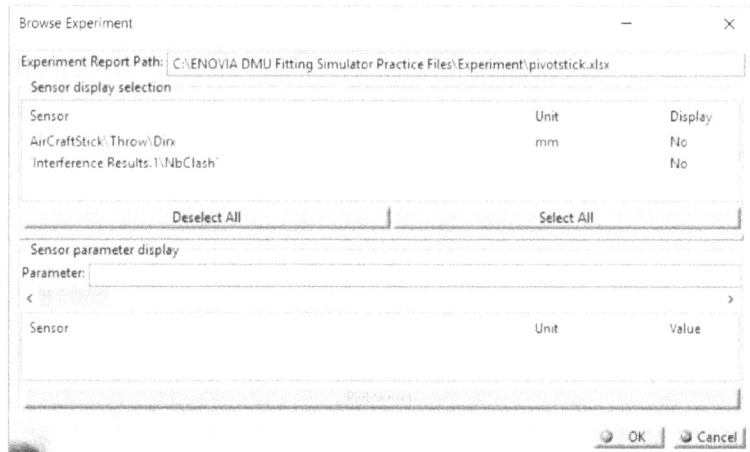

Figure 4–50

Design Considerations

There are two methods of displaying the results of an experiment for a sensor:

- Drag the slider bar to change the time step. When this is done, the system displays the value of the parameter at the current time step.

- Click **Plot Sensors** to graphically display the results of the sensor against time.

1. Select the **Interference Results.1\NbClash** parameter to add it to the *Sensor parameter display* field.

2. Click **Plot Sensors**. The system plots the clash results with respect to the time step, as shown in Figure 4–51.

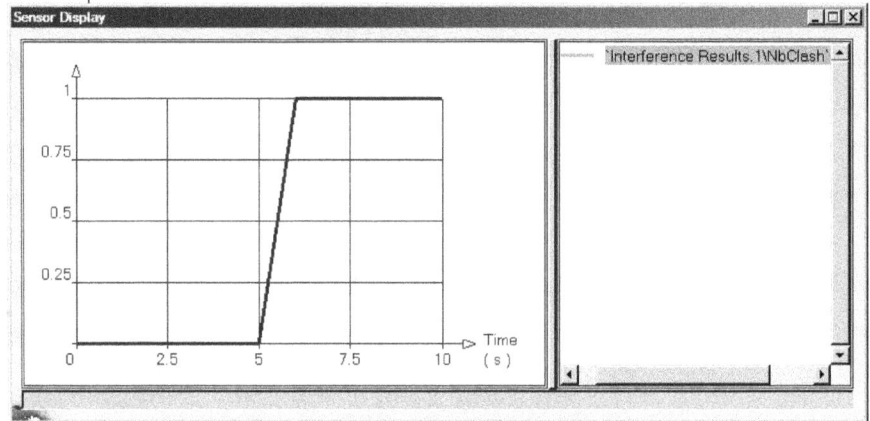

Figure 4–51

Design Considerations

The graph reports that only one clash condition exists and that it occurs at approximately five seconds. Although the system reports a clash condition, there is no information on where this clash is occurring. You can use two methods to determine the location of the clash:

- Move the track to a time step where the clash condition occurs and re-run the clash analysis.

- Create a swept volume and assemble the resulting CGR file into the assembly. A clash analysis could then be performed between the CGR and the assembly.

You will use the swept volume method in the next task.

3. Close the graph.

4. Click **Deselect All** to remove **Interference Results.1\NbClash** from the *Sensor time display* field.

5. Select the **AirCraftStick\Throw\Dirx** parameter.

6. In the *Parameter* field, enter **5** as shown in Figure 4–52. Press <Tab> to display the throw distance value at the start of the clash. The parameter value should be approximately 11.6mm.

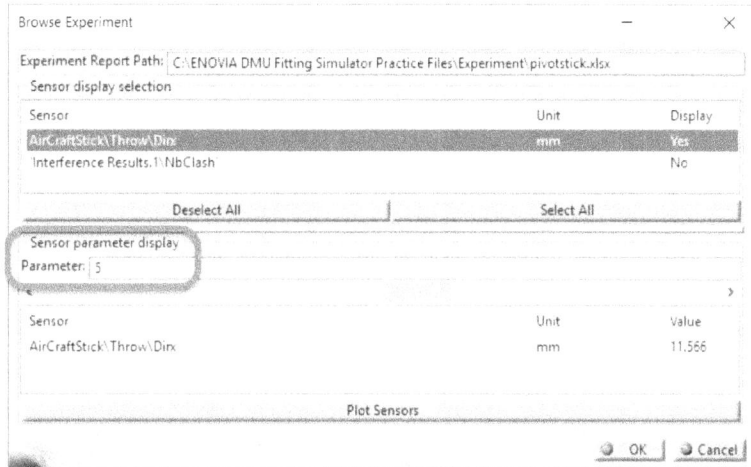

Browse Experiment

Experiment Report Path: C:\ENOVIA DMU Fitting Simulator Practice Files\Experiment\pivotstick.xlsx

Sensor display selection

Sensor	Unit	Display
AirCraftStick\Throw\Dirx	mm	Yes
Interference Results.1\NbClash		No

Deselect All	Select All

Sensor parameter display
Parameter: 5

Sensor	Unit	Value
AirCraftStick\Throw\Dirx	mm	11.566

Plot Sensors

OK   Cancel

Figure 4–52

7. Click **OK** to close the Browse Experiment window.

Task 6 - Create a swept volume and assemble it into the model.

In this task, you will create a swept volume of the **Stick** component.

1. In the DMU Simulation toolbar, click (Swept Volume). The Swept Volume dialog box opens as shown in Figure 4–53. Since only one track exists, the **Stick Pivot** track is automatically selected.

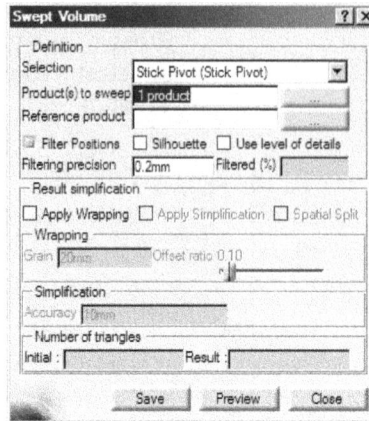

Figure 4–53

2. Click **Preview**. The system generates the swept shape and displays it in a Preview window, as shown in Figure 4–54.

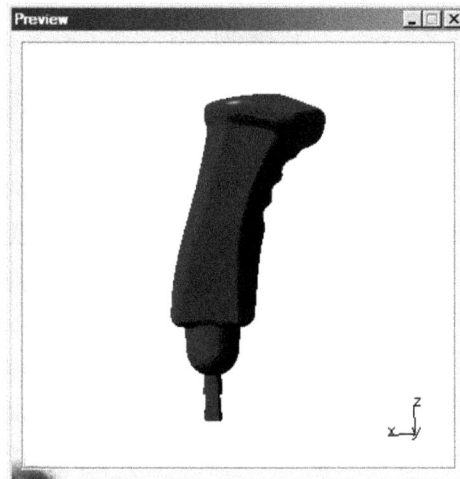

Figure 4–54

3. Click **Save** and save the CGR file with the default name and location.

4. Close the Swept Volume dialog box.

5. If time permits, continue with the next task.

Task 7 - (Optional) Assemble swept volume part.

1. Hide the **Stick** component.

2. Assemble the **Stick.1_SWEPTVOLUME.cgr** file into the **AirCraftStick** product. The assembly displays as shown in Figure 4–55.

Figure 4–55

Task 8 - (Optional) Run a clash analysis.

In this task, you will modify the previously created clash analysis to reference the CGR swept volume instead of the **Stick** component.

1. Modify the clash by double-clicking on it in the specification tree.

2. Select the **Selection 1** field. In the specification field, select **Stick**. This removes the component from the analysis.

3. Select **Stick.1_SWEPTVOLUME**.

4. Click **Apply** to re-run the analysis. The system indicates that the clash is occurring between the **Stick** and **Switch.2**.

5. Click **OK**.

6. Save the model and close the window.

www.ingramcontent.com/pod-product-compliance
Lightning Source LLC
Chambersburg PA
CBHW081543220326
41598CB00036B/6537